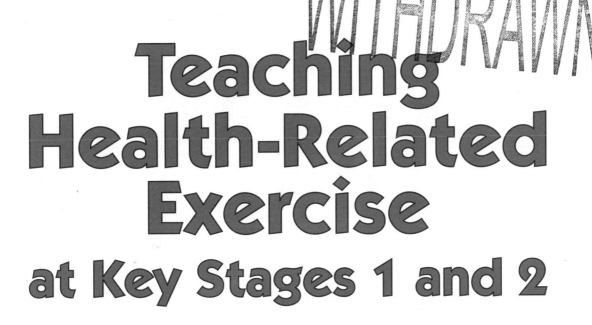

Teaching Health-Related Exercise
at Key Stages 1 and 2

Jo Harris, PhD
Loughborough University

Jill Elbourn, BH
Educational Exercise Consultant

11

Human Kinetics

Library of Congress Cataloging-in-Publication Data

Harris, Jo, 1955-
    Teaching health-related exercise at key stages 1 and 2 / Jo
Harris, Jill Elbourn.
      p.   cm.
    Includes bibliographical references (p.).
    ISBN 0-87322-666-6
    1. Physical education for children--Great Britain. 2. Exercise-
-Study and teaching (Elementary)--Great Britain. 3. Health
education--Great Britain. I. Elbourn, Jill, 1959-   . II. Title.
GV443.H317 1997   96-48338
372.86'0941--dc21   CIP

ISBN: 0-87322-666-6

Copyright © 1997 by Jo Harris and Jill Elbourn

Acquisitions Editor: Scott Wikgren
Developmental Editor: Elaine Mustain
Assistant Editor: Susan Moore-Kruse
Editorial Assistant: Amy Carnes
Copyeditor: Kathleen Lyle
Proofreader: Kathy Bennett
Graphic Designer: Judy Henderson
Graphic Artist: Yvonne Winsor
Photo Editor: Boyd LaFoon
Cover Designer: Judy Henderson
Photographer (cover): Jo Harris
Photographer: Jo Harris (taken at Rosebery Primary School)
Illustrator: Studio 2-D
Printer: Versa Press

Printed in the United States of America   10 9 8 7 6 5 4 3 2 1

Human Kinetics
Web site: http://www.humankinetics.com/

United States: Human Kinetics, P.O. Box 5076, Champaign, IL 61825-5076
1-800-747-4457
e-mail: humank@hkusa.com

Canada: Human Kinetics, Box 24040, Windsor, ON N8Y 4Y9
1-800-465-7301 (in Canada only)
e-mail: humank@hkcanada.com

Europe: Human Kinetics, P.O. Box IW14, Leeds LS16 6TR, United Kingdom
(44) 1132 781708
e-mail: humank@hkeurope.com

Australia: Human Kinetics, 57A Price Avenue, Lower Mitcham, South Australia 5062
(08) 277 1555
e-mail: humank@hkaustralia.com

New Zealand: Human Kinetics, P.O. Box 105-231, Auckland 1
(09) 523 3462
e-mail: humank@hknewz.com

Contents

List of Activities

Abbreviations

HRE Health-Related Exercise

KS Key Stage (National Curriculum)

NC National Curriculum (England and Wales)

PE Physical Education

Foreword

Over the past ten years there has been a gradual transformation in the belief that exercise and physical activity can bring about important health benefits. Many teachers have recognised the need to use their physical education programme to stimulate an interest in further participation, and acknowledged the considerable knowledge base involved in promoting safe and effective exercise. This recognition by teachers has come about through extensive in-service provision that Jo Harris and Jill Elbourn have undertaken throughout the whole country over the past seven years and the numerous articles, papers and booklets that they have generated.

Their impressive record in promoting a concern for health-related exercise has been instrumental to the success of the movement and has generated informed and intelligent practice with teachers. Their in-service courses and articles have always had a practical focus because they believe that teachers value tutors who lead by example and can provide genuine guides to practice—guides that teachers can use tomorrow morning with their classes.

It is this spirit that guides the present book—a book that provides genuine insights and practical action steps that teachers can incorporate into their teaching. Jo Harris and Jill Elbourn are fine exponents of this practical art and I am sure that all teachers will find strong support for their proposals. This is a much-needed book because it is comprehensive, very readable and provides a knowledge base that will lead to informed and intelligent practice.

Len Almond
Director of Exercise and Health Group and Senior Lecturer, Loughborough University
December 1996

Acknowledgements

We would like to express our appreciation to Len Almond who helped us to believe in our ability to assist others through in-service courses and the writing of teaching resources.

We would also like to thank colleagues, friends and children who have co-operated and provided us with opportunities to talk through and try out our ideas.

Further, we would like to acknowledge the staff and pupils of Rosebery Primary School, Loughborough, Leicestershire for their co-operation.

Introduction

We wrote this book for primary school teachers and primary school curriculum leaders for physical education. But having written it, we have realised it is a significant teaching resource for students, teachers, advisers and lecturers involved in primary school initial teacher training and INSET courses. It is also of interest to sports coaches and exercise teachers who are involved in teaching children in the 5 to 11 age range and to health promotion staff and individuals responsible for the health and physical well-being of children.

The National Curriculum (NC) formally recognises health-related exercise (HRE) as an essential element of the curriculum and it is important that this significant area of work is delivered effectively in schools. HRE is statutory at every key stage and forms a compulsory component of physical education and health education. As such, it highlights the importance and value of educating children about exercise throughout their schooling. Understanding why people exercise, undergoing positive exercise experiences, and learning to become independently active can help children to make informed decisions concerning exercise as an integral part of their lifestyle. This is especially important at a time when current research is highlighting the low activity levels of many children and raising awareness about the current and future health status of young people.

We wrote to help both non-specialist and specialist primary school teachers deliver the HRE component of the NC effectively. We included a variety of ways in which HRE can be organised and delivered within the curriculum, from topic-based cross-curricular work to focused units within physical education. We have also provided lesson examples which address the key issues of progression, differentiation and assessment.

In the text, we have incorporated the knowledge, understanding and skills essential to the promotion of active lifestyles and we wrote with the non-specialist particularly in mind. We have addressed the NC HRE requirements for both physical education and health education, and have considered whole-school approaches to health education.

Features of the Book

The book

- translates National Curriculum theory into practice,
- links the physical education and health education requirements,
- covers the essential theory in a straightforward manner for the non-specialist,
- has a practical orientation,
- contains practical lesson ideas using simple equipment,
- comprises a wide variety of teaching styles and workable assessment procedures, and
- is a flexible resource enabling teachers to determine the methods of delivery most appropriate for their pupils.

Chapter 1 begins with a consideration of children's activity and fitness levels and their state of health. Chapter 2 focuses on exercise recommendations and prescriptions for children and describes exercise practices and specific exercises that are and are not recommended. Chapter 3 outlines the National Curriculum requirements for HRE as specified for physical education and health education. Chapter 4 moves on to consider ways in which schools can support health-related initiatives. Chapters 5 and 6 contain detailed lesson examples for Key Stages 1 and 2 respectively. The final chapter gives point-by-point instructions for 19 activities which can be included in health-related PE lessons.

We suggest that teachers who are unfamiliar with the area of health-related exercise start by reading chapter 3 and follow this with chapters 5 or 6, whichever is most relevant to their particular key stage. Exercise teachers, sports coaches and health promotion staff who are not currently teaching in a school setting are advised to focus their reading on chapters 1, 2, 4 and 7. Chapter 4 is particularly relevant for teachers and health promotion staff who are interested in the area of activity promotion. Chapter 2 which focuses on safety will be of particular interest and importance to all individuals involved in the practical delivery of exercise to children aged 5 to 11.

1 Children and Exercise

How Healthy Are Children?

Most people agree that children of all ages should frequently take part in physical activities which use large muscle groups over a reasonably sustained period of time (Simons-Morton et al. 1988). Brisk walking, running, swimming, cycling, skipping, dancing or playing active games has numerous health benefits for children and adults (Fentem, Bassey and Turnbull 1988).

It may be surprising to know that young children have been found to have risk factors for coronary heart disease, such as elevated blood pressure and cholesterol levels. Over 69 percent of 12-year-old children had at least one modifiable risk factor for coronary heart disease, according to a survey in Northern Ireland (Boreham et al. 1992) and 14 percent of 12-year-olds exhibited three or more risk factors. Similarly, as many as 60 percent of 12-year-olds in the United States exhibited more than one modifiable adult risk factor for coronary heart disease (Berenson et al. 1980). These statistics justify concern about the level of potential coronary risk in school children.

Obesity is a health problem for children and adults. In North America, childhood obesity is the most common chronic illness in childhood (Bar-Or 1994). Almost half of the adult population in Britain is overweight, and this percentage is steadily increasing (Department of Health 1993, 1994; Sports Council and Health Education Authority 1992a, 1992b). Moreover, a study of over 600 11- to 16-year-old children in England revealed that about 10 percent of the girls and 13 percent of the boys could be classified as overweight, and the researchers concluded that this proportion is too high (Armstrong and Welsman 1994). Indeed, many overweight children become overweight or obese adults (Lefebre 1994).

The Effects of Exercise on Children's Health

Although few children suffer from chronic diseases such as coronary heart disease, some diseases have their origins in childhood (Bar-Or 1994; Malina and Bouchard 1991). Physical activity in childhood can play a vital role in reducing the development of risk factors for coronary heart disease, including elevated blood pressure, high cholesterol levels and obesity. Inactivity increases the risk of heart disease, back pain, overweightness and obesity, and weak and fragile bones. Indeed, physical inactivity is an established risk factor for coronary heart disease. Inactive people are almost twice as likely to suffer from heart disease as active people (Powell et al. 1987).

It can be difficult to separate the effects of physical activity on children from those associated with normal growth and maturation (Bar-Or 1994; Bouchard et al. 1993; Malina 1990, 1994; Malina and Bouchard 1991). However, appropriate physical activity during childhood can confer health benefits not just for the present but also for the future. In particular, an active childhood can

- increase bone density and, as a result, reduce the development of osteoporosis in adulthood,
- help regulate body fatness and, as a result, reduce the development of obesity, and
- help regulate blood pressure (especially among hypertensive adolescents).

In short, physical activity among children can help improve the functional capacity for daily living. Physically active and fit youngsters are leaner than children and adolescents who are sedentary and unfit.

According to Malina (1990), many people think preventive medicine should begin in childhood, starting with learning to maintain a physically active lifestyle and developing a positive attitude towards physical activity. The positive effects of exercise on children's health are so great that the medical world is keen to be associated with the promotion of activity for young people:

> The habit of exercise is most beneficial when acquired young. Since an interest in physical activity is most easily stimulated in childhood and youth, it is essential its value is appreciated both by local education authorities and government (Royal College of Physicians 1991, p. 28).

How Active Are Children?

It is difficult to establish accurately how active children are (Bar-Or 1990; Riddoch and Boreham 1995), but they are believed to be habitually more active than adults (Bar-Or 1993). However, researchers have found that children's levels of activity are generally lower than they anticipated and probably too low to gain health benefits. Their concern is that too little activity over time will contribute towards an increase in low-activity related (hypokinetic) conditions such as heart disease, osteoporosis and back pain. Morris (1988) believes that:

> For lack of exercise, we are bringing up a generation of children less healthy than it could be, and many of whom are likely to be at high risk in later life of serious disease and shortened life expectancy (p. 3).

One study (Sleap and Warburton 1992) found that primary-aged children in England took part in physical activity that was vigorous enough to make them sweaty or out of breath, but not for sustained periods of time. Less than half of the children took part in activity lasting as long as 10 minutes. Almost a quarter of PE lesson time was spent on inactive tasks such as standing, sitting, listening and queuing.

Another study monitoring the heart rate of primary school children (Armstrong and Bray 1991) found that few of them experienced the amount of exercise considered necessary for cardiovascular health (three 20-minute periods of exercise with a heart rate in excess of 139 beats per minute). Over a period of three days, only about 20 percent of the children had even one exercise period of this intensity. In fact, 25 percent of the girls and 19 percent of the boys did not have a single 10-minute exercise period of this intensity in three days. The children in this study were generally physically active only for periods of five minutes or so at a time.

A leading physical educator in England has concluded:

> The current level and pattern of children's physical activity is a cause for grave concern.

Physical educators at all levels of education must collaborate with each other and with the community and the home to meet this challenge. The future health of our children depends upon it (Armstrong 1990, p. 13).

Limited research has been carried out on this subject in Britain (Cale and Almond 1992a, 1992b), but the available results suggest that

- activity levels are lower than is desirable for health gains,
- girls are less active than boys, and
- activity levels decrease as children get older (Armstrong 1989; Armstrong et al. 1990a; Armstrong et al. 1990b; Armstrong and Bray 1991; Dickenson 1987; Northern Ireland Fitness Survey 1989; Sports Council for Wales 1987; Williams 1988).

Research also suggests that children are less active now than they used to be. A study on children's eating habits over a 50-year period demonstrated a reduction in food intake but little change in body mass. A major decrease in physical activity is the proposed explanation (Durnin 1992). There has been a significant decline in the freedom and choice for children (especially girls) to be independently active outside the home (Hillman et al. 1990). Many children spend hours engaged in sedentary activities such as watching the television, playing computer games, reading or studying. Television watching alone averages about 20 hours a week for British children aged between 4 and 15 (Central Statistical Office 1994).

Widespread car ownership has also contributed to the trend towards more sedentary lifestyles. Car journeys to school (as opposed to walking, cycling or travelling by public transport) doubled between 1975 (11 percent) and 1991 (22 percent). One possible reason for this is parental concern about the security of their children (Central Statistical Office 1994). Safety issues, such as hazardous road conditions and fear of assault, have led to real concerns about children walking or playing in public places and these issues must be addressed by public policy makers.

For many children, physical activity is not an integral part of everyday life. We need to find ways of increasing their activity levels. One possibility is to encourage children, where possible, to walk or cycle to school instead of coming by car or bus. Planned exercise sessions can also be incorporated into everyday school activities, and children should be provided with a range of accessible and attractive exercise opportunities. PE lessons in schools play a vital role in activating, educating and motivating children. For some children, these lessons might present the only regular opportunities for physical activity.

Childhood Activity and Adult Health

Inactive children tend to become inactive adults. People who exercise regularly in their youth are more likely to exercise in later years. A national survey revealed that 25 percent of those active at the ages of 14 to 19 were very active currently, compared with only 2 percent currently active who had been inactive at that earlier age (Sports Council and Health Education Authority 1992b). One of the main conclusions of the national survey was that:

> The foundation skills for sport, recreation and active living and understanding of the benefits of physical activity need to be learned at an early age (Sports Council and Health Education Authority 1992b, p. 11).

However, activity levels in childhood are not wholly reliable predictors of exercise habits in adulthood (Sallis 1994). One reason for this may be that some activities children are taught, such as team sports, are difficult to carry over into adult life. Schools should emphasise a wider range of physical activities for children to participate in and enjoy. Influencing health-related behaviour in positive ways early in life may have significant long-term pay-offs in terms of improved health and quality of life.

Fitness Testing

Although we often use the term 'fitness', it is complex to define and to measure. One definition is 'the ability to perform physical work satisfactorily' (World Health Organisation 1968, cited in Gauvin, Wall and Quinney 1994). Physical fitness includes health-related components such as

- cardiovascular endurance,
- flexibility,
- muscular endurance,
- muscular strength, and
- body composition

and skill-related or performance-related components such as

- agility,
- balance,
- co-ordination,
- power,
- reaction time, and
- speed.

Fitness for life differs from fitness for a particular sport. Measures of fitness are very specific to the different components being measured. For example, a timed shuttle run can give some measure of speed; timed curl-ups can indicate muscular strength and endurance of the abdominal muscles; and a 'sit and reach' test can measure flexibility of the lower back and back of upper leg (hamstring) muscles.

How Fit Are Children?

We often hear that children are not as fit these days as they used to be. Stories in the media have highlighted the lazy 'couch potato', implying that many of today's young people are unfit, fat and unhealthy. However, researchers who have compared children's fitness levels now with values recorded over past decades have found very little difference in the results (Armstrong 1989, 1990). Also, contrary to what you might expect, some children with high fitness test scores are very inactive and some children with low fitness test scores are very active.

Although fitness is an effective indicator of activity levels in adults, this is not necessarily the case for children. The fitness of children seems to be due to genetic factors, and fitness testing at a young age tends to measure inherited characteristics such as the efficiency of the heart and lungs which have had limited time to be affected by lifestyle habits. We should probably be less concerned with children's fitness scores than with their level of participation in physical activity. Furthermore, a firm link has yet to be established between children's fitness scores and health.

Should Children Be Tested for Fitness?

Some authorities have expressed concern over negative experiences such as exhausting testing procedures and public and unfair comparisons of scores in fitness testing programmes (Armstrong and Biddle 1992; Biddle and Biddle 1989; Harris and Elbourn 1994). Some testing procedures are inappropriate owing to varying stages of skeletal and biological maturation. Tests are often invalid and unreliable because of differing motivation among students. A leading exercise physiologist has stated that:

> Fitness tests simply determine the obvious, at best only distinguishing the mature child from the immature child (Armstrong 1990, p. 12).

Poor Testing Practices

The National Association for Sport and Physical Education in America (1992) provides the following examples of poor fitness testing practice:

- Testing once or twice a year simply because it is a required or expected procedure, or solely for the purpose of giving children awards.
- Testing without explaining the purpose of the tests or the implications of the individual results.
- Requiring children to perform tests without adequate practice and preparation.

Recommended Testing Practices

The aim of fitness testing is to develop and maintain motivation and promote participation, particularly amongst the least fit and less active children (American College of Sports Medicine 1988; Physical Education Association 1988). The main recommendations are the following:

- Focus on health-related aspects such as stamina, strength and suppleness rather than skill-related aspects such as speed and power.
- Emphasise personal involvement and improvement, not social comparison.
- Stimulate interest in learning about the effects of exercise.
- Increase understanding of health-related concepts.
- Encourage positive attitudes and a lifetime commitment to activity.

For children, the link between activity levels and health status appears to be stronger than the link between fitness and health (Fox 1991). The health benefits of physical activity are achieved by participating, not necessarily by achieving a high level of performance or physical fitness. It is the process of activity itself that has benefits, not the product of being good or better than someone else (Biddle and Biddle 1989).

What Do Children Think About Physical Activity?

Children like to be active because it is fun and enjoyable. This is more important to them than wanting to compete and win (Sports Council for Wales 1993). The enjoyment comes from a sense of achievement, challenge and excitement, and the opportunity to participate with friends (Wankel and Kreisel 1985). One of the strongest predictors of future activity is a perception of personal efficacy, or confidence regarding one's ability to be active on a regular basis (Sallis 1994).

A recent national survey in England of young people and sport (Sports Council 1995) informs us that

- 9 out of 10 children enjoy being involved in physical activity,
- 9 out of 10 children think it is 'important to keep fit', and
- 8 out of 10 children 'feel fit and healthy when being active'.

What Motivates Children to Be Active?

Girls generally prefer more individual activities than boys, who tend to find competitive games-based activities more enjoyable (Goudas and Biddle 1993). Obese children prefer activity that is 'easy' or 'steady' rather than vigorous, exhausting exercise (Epstein et al. 1991).

Reasons for children not choosing to become involved in activity include lack of confidence, limited success and boredom (Whitehead 1993) and lack of time (Sallis 1994). Children who are considered 'above average' in ability in PE are much more likely to be active in later life (Kuh and Cooper 1992). This is probably a result of the positive experiences of these above-average children in PE classes (McGeorge, Almond and Hawkins 1995). These issues highlight the importance of delivering positive physical education and allowing all pupils to succeed and progress at their own level and to feel competent and confident in an exercise environment.

How Schools Can Promote Activity

To promote an active lifestyle for children, we should emphasise task-oriented goals—accomplishing an individual achievable task—rather than ego-oriented tasks—trying to be better than someone else (Duda 1994). Emphasis on task-oriented goals is linked to greater enjoyment of physical activity (Duda, Fox, Biddle and Armstrong 1992). Task orientation within a physical education or sporting environment emphasises that

- being the best is doing your best,
- how you play is as important as winning and losing,
- mistakes are part of learning and improving,
- everyone, regardless of ability, has something to offer and receive,
- success is a product of trying hard rather than possessing superior talent, and
- working with, rather than always outdoing others, is a valuable experience (adapted from Duda 1994, p. 126).

How Families Can Promote Activity

Parents play an influential role in the activity levels and patterns of their children. Studies of 9- to 13-year-old children reveal that parents support children's physical activity through

- serving as role models (although most parents do not model regular physical activity),
- providing encouragement, and
- directly helping children to be active by participating in activities with their children, organising activities, or transporting children to places where they can be active (Sallis 1994).

A better understanding of the complex mechanisms of family influence will help us to improve the promotion of physical activity for all family members in the future (Taylor, Baranowski and Sallis 1994).

How Much Exercise Should Children Do?

We do not yet know just how much activity children and adolescents need in order to gain health benefits. Indeed, Bar-Or (1993) has suggested that, as a rule, children do not require exercise prescriptions, since they are generally more habitually active than adults or adolescents. However, recent guidelines for children suggest the following prescription which is generally considered to promote short-term, and enhance future, health and well-being:

- Children should, at a minimum, be active three or more times a day.
- The level of activity should be moderately intense, alternating bouts of activity with rest or easier activity as necessary.

• The activity time should be enough to use at least three to four kilocalories per kilogram of body weight per day. This is the energy expenditure involved in 30 minutes or more of active play or moderate sustained activity which may be distributed over three or more activity sessions per day.

• The types of physical activity recommended are childhood games and lifestyle activities such as walking and cycling to school.

All young people should be able to achieve this minimum level of activity. The guidelines also recommend an optimal level of activity representing a further goal for those who have achieved the minimum standard. It should include

• three or more sessions of exercise daily, totalling 60 minutes (at least six kilocalories per kilogram of body weight per day) and

• moderate to vigorous active play or moderate sustained activity (with rest if necessary), including weight-bearing exercise such as games playing or dancing (adapted from Corbin, Pangrazi and Welk 1994, p.7).

Five- to seven-year-old children have limited physical capacities and attention span. It is inappropriate to expect them to engage in lengthy, continuous periods of moderate to vigorous activity.

Shorter bouts of activity repeated frequently are more 'natural' for young children (Bar-Or 1993). This is consistent with the proposed recommendations for children which acknowledge the potential health benefits of sporadic activity.

The recommendations for adolescents incorporate physical activities which last 20 minutes or more at a time, so for children nine years old and over it is a good idea to move gradually towards exercise such as 10 to 15 minutes of brisk walking, easy jogging or cycling.

These recommendations should be applied with common sense and sensitivity, the simple aim being to encourage every child to be more active more often, without being too precise about specific requirements. Cale and Harris (1993) emphasise the following points:

• Activity recommendations should be regarded as guidelines rather than strict rules or rigid prescriptions.

• All children, irrespective of gender, ethnicity or disability can benefit from physical activity.

• The initial aim is to gradually increase children's activity levels from their current levels.

• Progress should be gradual and at a level and pace that suits the individual child.

• Children should be introduced to a broad range of activities over time.

- Young children may prefer frequent bouts of sporadic activity to sustained activity sessions.
- Physical activity experiences should be positive, achievable and enjoyable.
- Children should be made aware of activity opportunities at school, around the home, and within the local community.
- Children who maintain the minimum standard can be gradually moved towards the optimal activity goals (involving longer and more energetic activity).
- Children should be helped to develop behavioural skills (such as considering ways of fitting activity into their life, overcoming barriers to activity, rewarding activity behaviour) which will help them to maintain involvement in an active lifestyle during adolescence and young adulthood.

Exercise guidelines can be helpful for parents, teachers and coaches because they provide a way of judging whether children are active enough. It is important however, that children are encouraged and coaxed into increasing their activity levels, rather than being forced which is likely to be counter-productive in the long term. Adults who felt that they were forced to exercise during their pre-teen years tended to be relatively inactive as adults (Taylor et al. 1993). Winning the war of lifetime health is a much greater priority than winning the battle of short-term fitness.

Key Points

- Health-related exercise (HRE) is about knowledge, understanding, skills and attitudes.
- The positive benefits of exercise for children are well established.
- Physical inactivity is a risk factor for heart disease.
- Girls are less active than boys, and activity levels decline with age.
- Fitness testing should be positive, motivating and educational.
- Active children are more likely to become active adults.
- School PE has an important role to play in laying the foundation for an active lifestyle.

2 *Safe Exercise for Children*

How Children Respond to Exercise

Children do not respond to exercise in the same way as adults (Bar-Or 1993, 1994; Zwiren, 1988). These differences are discussed below, along with their implications for teachers and coaches.

Mechanical Efficiency

Children are less mechanically efficient than adults. They produce more heat, and tire out more easily in prolonged high-intensity events such as middle and long distance running, swimming and cycling. When walking or running at a given speed, children use more oxygen than adults.

- Avoid subjecting children to prolonged high-intensity exercise such as running, swimming or cycling fast over long distances, or sustained high-intensity efforts such as continuous jumping.

Physiological Efficiency

Children have a higher heart rate than adults, a lower stroke volume (amount of blood leaving the heart on each beat) and a higher, more shallow, breathing rate. Their lungs are less efficient, so they cannot extract as much oxygen from the air as adults and, in effect, have to work harder to get oxygen. Breathing hard also increases the rate at which the body loses water. For these reasons children become more quickly and easily fatigued early in high-intensity tasks such as fast running, swimming, cycling and jumping. Unlike adults, children under the age of 10 are unlikely to significantly improve their aerobic ability through training.

- Be aware of children's physiological limitations and avoid continuous high-intensity tasks. Instead, encourage intermittent activities with appropriate periods of rest or reduced-intensity exercise (such as walking or easy jogging).

Anaerobic Ability

Children have less carbohydrate stored in their muscles than adults do, and a reduced ability to use it for energy. This means that children's ability to perform intense explosive anaerobic tasks that last 10 to 90 seconds (such as running events of 100 metres, 200 metres or 400 metres) is much lower than that of adults. However, children reach steady-state exercise and recover more quickly from it than adults, so intermittent activities suit them very well.

- Avoid involving children in a continuous series of fast or powerful tasks, or bursts of strenuous activity (as in short-repetition, high-intensity training). Encourage intermittent activities (such as relays) with appropriate periods of rest or active recovery (such as walking, easy jogging). Before adolescence, children are better equipped for aerobic activity than for anaerobic activity.

Heat Regulation

Children have an immature cardiovascular system and cannot bring heat to the surface very efficiently when exercising in hot weather. They also have a higher ratio of body surface area to weight, a lower rate of sweat production, and a higher rate of heat production during exercise. They heat up rapidly during exercise, and overheat more easily in hot weather. In cold weather children lose heat more quickly and can easily become very cold.

- In hot weather, encourage children to wear light-weight clothing. Reduce the exercise intensity, provide frequent rest periods, and have plenty of fluids available. In hot climates, young sports performers involved in training programmes require a long and gradual period of acclimatisation. In cold weather, ensure that children are adequately clothed with plenty of layers and are kept actively involved so that they do not become very cold.

Growth Patterns

Children have weaker bones than adults. The growth plate cartilage at the ends of the bones is particularly susceptible to injury. Because children grow in spurts, with non-linear growth patterns, their body proportions are not the same as those of adults. Muscle growth occurs later than bone growth, leading to a higher risk of overuse injuries.

- Avoid prolonged high-impact moves such as deep knee landings from jumps and deep squats (including 'bunny jumps' and 'duck walking'). Ballistic (bouncing) stretching should also be avoided because the growth plate is susceptible to injury from muscles repeatedly pulling bones at their ends. Children tend to be bottom heavy, with a weak upper body. They should not be asked to perform 'adult' exercises such as full-length push-ups because their relatively weak mid-section will struggle to manage their body weight. The use of external weights is not advisable. Tasks should be differentiated so that children can achieve success at their own level. Short static (held) stretches and modified (low-level, easy) strengthening exercises are recommended.

Perception of Effort

Children perceive exercise at a given intensity to be easier than adults, because they do not feel the stress of exercise as acutely as adults. They often feel ready to continue after a short rest, as their aerobic system provides a faster recovery.

- Children may say that exercise feels easier than it actually is. As well as asking them how they feel, look out for signs and symptoms of discomfort and fatigue. Do not allow children to over-commit themselves. On occasions, the exercise may have to be stopped earlier than the children would like.

Although children have the advantage over adults of generally being lighter in weight and having more elastic bones, they are at a disadvantage because

- they are more active and less wise,
- their skeleton is changing shape and size, and
- they have relatively weak growth plates near the ends of their bones (King 1995).

The main reasons for limiting children's involvement in 'adult' sporting events, such as marathons, are their low economy of movement and thermo-regulatory limitations (American Academy of Pediatrics 1983).

Appropriate Exercises for Children

There are lot of exercises that children can perform safely, but there are also some that should be avoided in PE lessons.

Which Exercises Are Safe for Children?

Activities can involve any combination of walking, running, jumping, travelling, throwing, catching, passing, lifting, carrying, and lowering. Exercises designed for children should cater for a wide range of developmental ages and physical abilities. Differentiated tasks are important, because there can be as much as four years' difference in developmental age between children of the same chronological age (Lee 1987). Children should be offered a choice of pace, style, equipment or distance so that they are able to carry out a given task at their own level.

Developmentally appropriate strength-related exercises such as low-level curl-ups and push-ups should be offered at a variety of levels so that all pupils can achieve success. Easier exercises involving short levers and reduced body weight, such as push-ups against a wall or from a box position on the floor, are easier than starting from a full-length body position.

Children should have appropriate footwear (such as cushioned trainers) for activities which involve them repeatedly supporting their body weight, like running, jumping, skipping and games playing. Footwear should provide support and protection for growing bones. Knee pain and some specific

CAN CHILDREN DO TOO MUCH EXERCISE?

Most children are unlikely to experience overuse injuries, although they are becoming more common in children who take part in sporting activities from an early age (Maffulli 1995). Talented children who are involved in regular training schedules may be at risk, especially if the amounts of training are excessive or designed for adult athletes. Teachers and coaches need to be fully aware that children are more susceptible to overuse injury than adults (Micheli 1986).

Risks can occur when

- there are abrupt changes in the amount or level of training,
- strength and flexibility work are not evenly balanced,
- joints are placed under stress due to poor alignment, and
- inappropriate footwear is worn and the training surface is hard (Zwiren 1988).

Fortunately, most of these injuries are minor and short-lived. According to a Sports Council study, youth sports are relatively safe (Rowley 1992). The study found that the type, location and severity of the injuries varied in different sports. Fifteen percent of the young people studied sustained overuse injuries, although the specific causes were not clear. The report reminded parents and coaches that young athletes are particularly prone to overuse injuries during growth spurts, and that this risk can be minimised by reducing or modifying training programmes.

When designing training programmes for children, it is important to

- increase the intensity of the training gradually, by not more than 10 percent per week,
- ensure that work on muscular strength and flexibility is adequate and balanced,
- teach and insist on good technique,
- ensure the use of comfortable supportive footwear and appropriate running surfaces (preferably soft surfaces such as grass to minimise impact injuries), and
- take appropriate precautions with respect to weather conditions (American College of Sports Medicine 1991).

Girls undergoing heavy training programmes are at risk of developing osteopenia. This condition, also known as hypo-oestrogenism, is characterised by low levels of the hormone oestrogen (Warren 1980). Young female athletes with low body fat levels typically have low oestrogen levels, resulting in an absent or disrupted menstrual cycle. Oestrogen is critical in the development and maintenance of bone density and low levels of it tend to be associated with skeletal injuries such as stress fractures. Osteopenia is only likely to be a serious risk for highly competitive girls, such as dancers, gymnasts and distance runners.

Training and performance levels should take into account the chronological and biological age of the child and their physical and psychological immaturity (Maffulli 1995). Well-intended but misdirected parents and coaches can put pressure on children who may be uncomfortable with the rigours of competitive activity (Micheli and Klein 1991).

injuries are often associated with excessive amounts of high-impact activities such as running and jumping on hard surfaces without adequate supportive footwear (Grisogono 1984).

Which Exercises Should Be Avoided?

Children are not miniature adults. They should only be involved with sporting events that are appropriate for their developmental age. Children should not be pushed into competitive events too early (National Association for Sport and Physical Education 1992) or into full-sized adult versions of games. The National Coaching Foundation (Lee 1987) emphasises that the sport or activity should fit the child and that competitive structures should be tailored to the needs of children, not adults.

Some exercises that were common in the past, such as toe touching and straight leg sit-ups, are now considered to be potentially damaging. They may do more harm than good (Donovan, McNamara and Gianoli 1989; London Central

YMCA 1994). Unsafe exercises can cause immediate injury or long-term damage. Exercises that may cause problems are those involving hyperextension (extreme extension or arching) or hyperflexion (extreme flexion or bending) of a joint; or those involving uncontrolled, rapid movements. These exercises stress the muscles, tendons, ligaments and connective tissue, which may result in long-term damage to joints and a subsequent restriction of physical activity. The areas of the body that are particularly susceptible to damage are the neck, the knee and the back. Examples of unsafe exercises are presented in table 2.1.

Exercises performed with poor technique may cause injury or discomfort. Examples are skipping and astride jumps performed with knees turned inwards or with stiff knees, and landing on toes only. This puts undue strain on knee ligaments and shins. Both activities can be health-promoting providing that they are performed with knees bending over the ankles and weight being taken from the balls of the feet through to the heels on landing.

	TABLE 2.1	Problem Exercises and Safe Alternatives	
Body part	**Problem exercise**	**Risk**	**Safe alternatives**
Neck	Full head circling (to mobilise neck)	Damage to the small bones in the top of the spine	Controlled turning and tilting of the head to each side; half circles of head (forwards only)
Knee	Hurdle stretch (to stretch hamstrings)	Stress placed on the outside of the knee of the bent leg and on the hip joint and spine	'Sit and reach' stretch with both legs straight (or with one leg bent and foot flat), hands on floor and leaning forwards
	Deep knee bends (to and from jumps)	Stress placed on the ligaments inside the knee joint	Controlled landings with knee angle at least 90 degrees (therefore, not so deep)
Back	Standing toe touching (to stretch hamstrings)	Stress placed on the bones in the lower back	'Sit and reach' stretch with both legs straight (or with one leg bent and foot flat), hands on floor and leaning forwards
	Straight-leg sit-ups (to strengthen abdominals)	Stress placed on the bones in the lower back	Bent-knee curl-ups with lower back pressed firmly into the supporting mat

Sporting events or training sessions which require explosive movements with rapid acceleration and deceleration of body parts, or which involve continuous impact (such as rebounding and vigorous throwing) are considered potentially harmful to children (Lee 1987). A summary of the issues associated with problem exercises is presented in table 2.2.

Beginning and Ending Exercise Sessions

It is important that children should ease into exercise and help the body to recover afterwards by performing warm-ups and cool-downs.

Warming Up

Warming up is essential for safe exercise and can easily be incorporated into your PE routine.

Why Do Children Need to Warm Up?

A warm-up helps children to prepare their bodies gradually for activities to follow. Just as it is advisable to go up through the gears of a car or bike steadily, so it is wise to ease the body gradually into exercise. Going straight into top gear or overdrive will place undue pressure on the body and may result in discomfort and early fatigue. An effective warm-up should prepare the mind and body for activity, help prevent injury, and may improve performance (Alter 1988).

Easing into exercise makes the exercise experience more comfortable and reduces the likelihood of injury such as muscle strains. Although children do not often pull muscles during activity, it is important that good habits are established early. Children should learn from a young age that stretching warm muscles is an important preparation for activity. Safe involvement in positive exercise experiences is vital in effectively promoting both

TABLE 2.2 Problems Caused by Unsafe Exercises

Issue	Description	Example	Problem	Solution
Inappropriate use of momentum	Movements performed at speed	Wildly swinging arms around the body	Potential to strain muscles, tendons, ligaments	Perform all exercises at a pace that can be controlled
Ballistic stretching	Repetitive bouncing of muscles at the end of their range	Bouncing in 'sit and reach' hamstring stretch	Causes tiny muscle tears and muscle stiffness and soreness	Hold stretches still for at least 6 to 10 seconds
Poor alignment	Placing and moving joints in anatomically undesirable positions	Deep knee bends and hurdle stretch position	Strains the ligaments of the joint creating instability	Ensure that joints are moved in safe and correct ways
Lack of stability	Performing exercises from unbalanced starting positions	Standing quads stretch; calf stretch with feet 'on a tightrope'	Ineffective stretch and loss of control of the exercise	Ensure a stable base of support (e.g., feet wide in calf stretch; use of wall/partner for quads stretch)
Excessive high-impact work	Performing continuous 'high-energy, jumping up and down' activities	Continuous tuck jumps or astride jumps	Prolonged stress on the weight-bearing joints	Ensure a mix of impacts, good landing technique and supportive footwear
Inappropriate use of isometric exercises	Performing static (i.e., 'held') strength exercises	Pushing hands one against the other; 'wall sit' exercise	Increase in blood pressure; limited strength gains over a small range of movement	For more effective strength/endurance gains, use isotonic (moving) exercises

short-term and long-term participation in physical activity. Children are not likely to enjoy a PE lesson if they have to rush into uncomfortable exercises that may result in stiff aching muscles.

What Should Be Included in a Warm-Up?

The range of activities that can be used in the warm-up session includes mobility exercises, pulse-raising or warming activities, and short, static muscle stretches.

- **Mobility exercises** are controlled movements of the joints to be used in the main activity (such as arm circles, side bends, knee lifts). These exercises warm and circulate fluid within the joints, allowing freer movement and preparing them for activity. Uncontrolled flinging exercises should be discouraged, because there is a risk of injuries being caused by muscles taken to the ends of their range of movement, at speed, while they are still cold.
- **Pulse-raising** or **warming activities** (such as walking, jogging, skipping, sidestepping, marching) raise the body's temperature. These activities prepare the cardiovascular system (heart, lungs, blood vessels) by gradually increasing the heart and breathing rate. This results in an increased supply of oxygen to the muscles, which become warmer as they are working. Children should not be asked to perform very vigorous

activities such as sprinting and continuous jumping until the body is thoroughly warm and suitable stretching has been performed.

- **Stretching** relevant muscles helps to prepare them to be lengthened safely and helps to prevent injuries such as 'pulled' or strained muscles. The warm-up should include short static stretches of the muscles which are to be used in the main activity, such as the back of the lower leg (calf) muscles for running activities, the front of the upper leg (thigh or quadriceps) muscles for jumping activities. Each stretch should be held still for 6 to10 seconds. Children who are not familiar with stretches should hold them for only a short time initially and gradually increase this time as they become more familiar with the positions.

Choose the mobility and pulse-raising activities within a warm-up based on the activity that will follow. For example, a football warm-up should contain simple activities relevant to the theme of the lesson (such as finding space, accurate passing, marking). This helps to set the focus for the lesson and to prepare the children psychologically. The mobility and pulse-raising activities can be interspersed. They can be performed in any order, and for time efficiency, can be combined (such as circling the shoulders whilst walking or jogging). The stretching can only be performed safely when the

Side bends

muscles are warm and should always come after pulse-raising or warming activities (Alter 1988).

Cooling Down

Cooling down is as important as warming up, and it is just as easy to incorporate into the PE lesson.

Why Children Need to Cool Down

A cool-down helps children to prepare their bodies gradually to stop exercising and helps to reduce stiff aching muscles. Going straight from top gear to first gear is stressful for a car and can be just as uncomfortable for the human body. A cool-down allows for a gradual recovery from energetic exercise.

Cool-downs are especially important after very vigorous exercise such as sprinting or jumping. Children can become dizzy, faint, or nauseated if they do not slow down or ease off gradually. A cool-down helps to slow the circulation to a steady rate and to disperse any waste products that have built up in the muscles (such as lactic acid which causes fatigue) (Alter 1988).

If the main activity did not include fast, vigorous exercise, specific pulse-lowering exercises may not be needed. The walk or jog from the activity area back to the changing rooms serves the purpose of keeping the main leg muscles moving, which assists blood circulation and disperses waste products that may have built up in the muscles. For example, after a games lesson outside, pupils could be asked to jog or walk quickly back to the changing rooms and then to do one or two leg stretches. This represents good practice as it incorporates pulse-lowering and stretching of the main muscles involved in the previous activity.

What Should Be Included in a Cool-Down?

The cool-down should include pulse-lowering or cooling activities. Muscle stretches are again useful.

- Pulse-lowering or cooling activities should gradually decrease in intensity (such as gentle jogging, walking, and simple mobility exercises such as knee lifts). This allows the heart rate and breathing rate to decrease gradually and comfortably, and assists the blood circulation and the removal of waste products from the muscles. This part of the cool-down is particularly important after energetic or vigorous activities such as sprinting and jumping.
- Muscle stretching helps to maintain flexibility so that the muscles do not become 'tight', and it helps to reduce any aches and pains. The cool-down should include longer static stretches of the muscles used in the main activity: for example, the chest (pectorals) and back of upper arm (triceps)

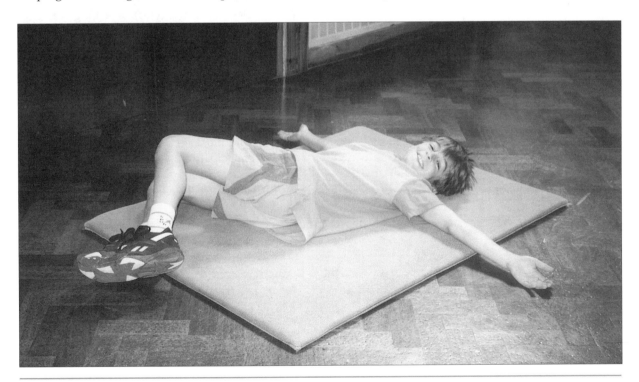

Obliques stretch

muscles after throwing activities; the back of the lower leg (calf) and the front of the upper leg (thigh or quadriceps) muscles after running and jumping activities. Each stretch should be held still for 10 to 12 seconds. As with the warm-up, pupils who are not familiar with stretches should hold stretches for only a short time initially and gradually increase this time as they become more familiar with the positions.

The main teaching points for recommended stretches are detailed in table 2.3.

Warming Up and Cooling Down

The NC for PE states that a warm-up and a cool-down should be integral parts of every lesson (Department for Education and the Welsh Office Education Department 1995). The warm-up should be viewed as the lead in to the lesson and the cool-down as the concluding activity.

- The warm-up in the first 5 to 10 minutes of the lesson provides a valuable opportunity to recap and revise prior skills and knowledge, and to introduce new movement ideas, which are to be developed later in the lesson.
- Use the cool-down in the last few minutes of the lesson to recap and summarise the main focus of the lesson, and to assess pupils' understanding.

Teachers of PE have an important role to play in educating children about exercise. If children are used to a warm-up at the start of every lesson and a cool-down at the end, they are much more likely to continue this procedure when participating in physical activity outside school.

- At KS 1, the pupils learn through teacher-led activities that a warm-up and cool-down are always performed at the beginning and end of an exercise session (see chapter 5).

- At KS 2, pupils become more familiar with the components of a warm-up and cool-down and are given opportunities to follow good practice and to be involved in demonstrating part of these procedures for general activities (see chapter 6).

As pupils move from KS 2 and through KS 3 and 4, they should progress from dependence on the teacher to increasing independence, gradually taking more responsibility for planning and performing their own warm-ups and cool-downs.

Warming up and cooling down can be taught through the activity areas at KS 1 and 2. The activity should be varied, fun, and active for all participants. The necessary knowledge, understanding and skills can be imparted gradually throughout the key stages, introducing limited new material at any one time. It is important that children should not come to regard warm-ups and cool-downs as boring barriers to the real action.

- Warm-up activities should be simple and easy to organise, so that participants are quickly involved in activity rather than standing around listening to long explanations.
- In cold conditions, it is important for children to be active as soon as possible. Ensure that the warm-up is continuous and active. Avoid long series of isolated mobility exercises (such as arm circles and hip circles) or a long series of held stretches. Instead, where possible, pulse-raising and mobility exercises can be combined (shoulder circles while walking) and a few relevant stretches can be interspersed with pulse raising.
- Children can wear layers of clothing during the warm-up, which can be removed for the main activity and replaced before the cool-down.
- Active participation by the teacher can be motivating and can help pupils gauge the pace and performance quality required.

	TABLE 2.3 *Recommended Stretches*			
Muscle(s)	**Actions using these muscles**	**Stretches**		**Teaching points**
Calf muscle (gastrocnemius)	Walking, jogging, running, skipping			Both feet facing forwards, feet apart (not on a 'tightrope'), back leg straight, heel down, back straight
Back of upper leg muscles (hamstrings)	Kicking, jogging, running			Standing: head, shoulders and backside lifted to avoid pressure on lower back
				Sitting: thigh to chest (not nose to knee)
Front of upper leg muscles (quadriceps)	Jumping, running, step-ups, kicking			Knees close together, push the foot into the hand (not foot into backside), hips forward
Inner thigh or groin muscles (adductors)	Games playing			Sitting: apply gentle pressure on inside of legs, lean forwards slightly, back straight, head and shoulders lifted
				Standing: hips forwards, feet flat, bend knee over ankle
Lower back and backside muscles (erector spinae and gluteus maximus)	Running, bending, straightening			Lengthen lower back, relax head and shoulders
Chest muscles (pectorals)	Catching, throwing, push-ups			Press shoulders back, lift the elbows, keep arms bent and back straight
Whole body	Any exercise activity	Standing		Breathe normally, reach as far as possible
Whole body	Any exercise activity	Sitting		Breathe normally, reach as far as possible
Whole body	Any exercise activity	Lying		Breathe normally, reach as far as possible

WARM-UP AND COOL-DOWN REMINDERS

Do	Don't
Involve everyone in activity at the same time.	Have individuals inactively waiting around for their turn.
Perform exercises with control.	Permit flinging, uncontrolled actions.
Progress gradually (go up steadily through the 'gears').	Rush too quickly into fast, rapid activities (such as sprints, jumps, relay races, vigorous tag games).
Ensure that muscles are warm before they are stretched.	Stretch cold muscles.
Hold stretches still.	Bounce in stretches.
Exercise at a comfortable, steady level.	Exercise so hard that you have to stop.
Exercise at your own pace.	Try and compete with others.
Maintain a straight, 'tall' back during exercises.	Perform exercises in which the back is arched.
Ensure that the knees turn out over the ankles during knee bends and that there is always at least 90 degrees (a right angle) between the lower and upper leg.	Perform deep knee bends or exercises with incorrect knee alignment (e.g., the knee twisted inwards or outwards).
Perform neck mobility exercises with care to avoid trapping nerves or damaging the small bones of the upper spine.	Perform exercises in which the head is forced forwards or backwards.
Where possible, mix impacts and teach and insist on safe technique for high-impact activities to minimise joint injuries.	Perform continuous high-impact activities (i.e., 'bouncing up and down' or jumping activities).

Exercises for Muscles, Bones and Joints

Exercise has beneficial effects for muscles, bones and joints. Appropriate exercises should be included in PE lessons.

Do Children Need to Do Flexibility Work?

Flexibility work involves performing exercises which maintain or increase the range of movement around joints, such as mobility exercises and stretching exercises. Mobility exercises involve controlled

Lower back stretch

ing a muscle or group of muscles still. Bouncing in stretches (ballistic stretching) is potentially harmful and not recommended in general use. Flexibility in the hip region and the lower back may help in the prevention of future back pain and postural defects. Flexibility can also help in the prevention of injury such as pulled or strained muscles, and may improve performance: it can help a performer to throw or kick further (Alter 1988).

Up to the age of about 11, children tend to have good flexibility and rarely strain muscles (Alter 1988). For the vast majority of primary school children it is acceptable that they

movement of joints through their normal range (such as shoulder circles, knee lifts and hip circles). Stretching exercises involve lengthening and hold-

- have some understanding of what flexibility is and how exercise improves flexibility,
- experience mobility (joint) exercises in warm-ups, and
- experience short held stretches in warm-ups and cool-downs.

If flexibility gains are needed, three sets of static stretches of 6 to 10 seconds duration should be performed at least every other day (Armstrong and Biddle 1992).

Seated whole-body stretches

FLEXIBILITY EXERCISES FOR TALENTED CHILDREN

Concentrating on flexibility exercises may only be necessary for talented performers who are undergoing training programmes for particular sports such as gymnastics, dance or swimming. It does appear to be beneficial for talented children to increase their joint flexibility before puberty, providing that this is carried out safely and effectively. Damage to joints must be avoided. Excessive flexibility may lead to joint instability and future health problems. The younger the athlete, the more important it is that only slow static stretching is utilised (McNaught-Davis 1986).

Should Children Do Strength Exercises?

Muscular strength is the amount of force a muscle (or group of muscles) can exert against a resistance (such as lifting a heavy bag or box). Muscular endurance is the ability of a muscle (or group of muscles) to work against a resistance repeatedly (such as carrying a bench or performing 10 continuous curl-ups). Strength can be improved through a variety of weight-bearing activities including whole-body activities, exercises for specific body parts, and the use of resistance equipment (such as elastics) and weights (such as dumbbells, barbells, and fixed machines).

Weight-bearing activities are those in which the body has to support all or part of its own weight (such as walking, running, jumping, dance and gymnastic activities) or support the weight of additional objects (such as a bat, ball or bean bag). Children benefit from being involved in weight-bearing activities—it helps to strengthen their bones. Running and jumping activities help to strengthen the lower body, and throwing, catching and striking activities help to strengthen the upper body. Primary school children should be involved in a wide range of weight-bearing activities for both the upper and lower body.

It is not necessary for children aged five to nine years to perform specific strength training exercises. However, towards the end of KS 2, children can be involved in simple low-level strength exercises, which involve controlling their own body weight rather than lifting external weights. It is important to focus on body parts that are not so much used in familiar weight-bearing activities, such as walking

and running. Examples of such body parts are the muscles in the tummy area (abdominals), the back and backside, and the chest and arms. Examples of appropriate low-level exercises are:

- easy tummy curls for the abdominal muscles (with hands on the floor or on the thighs),
- easy leg raises for the backside muscles (against a wall or from lying on front, legs lifted one at a time, head down),

Tummy curls

SHOULD CHILDREN TRAIN WITH WEIGHTS?

Both before and after puberty, girls and boys can achieve strength gains from training with weights (Kraemer and Fleck 1993). The possible benefits include injury prevention, improved posture, and protection against future back pain and osteoporosis (Rowland 1990). There is little risk of injury in an appropriate, supervised resistance training programme.

Training with heavy weights should be avoided with young children. Older children can be involved in performing about 8 to 12 repetitions of an exercise up to the point of muscle fatigue, gradually progressing from one set to three sets, no more than three times a week (with at least one day's rest between sessions). Each session should consist of one exercise for each major muscle group.

Talented children undergoing training programmes for particular sports can participate safely in properly designed progressive strength training programmes, with close adult supervision (American College of Sports Medicine 1991). However, as training is very specific, it is important for children to use the motor skills involved in a particular event rather than, or in addition to, just lifting weights (Jones and Mills 1995).

The following general recommendations have been made:

- Before puberty, children should only lift light weights (low resistance) (Rowland 1990).
- Children should not train with weights that they cannot lift 7 to 10 times (Fleck and Kraemer 1987).
- In the setting of a school lesson, weight training can be safely performed by children aged 13 to 14 years and over (Biddle 1991).
- Lifting maximal weights (as much as is possible) is inappropriate for children younger than 16 to 17 years (Fleck and Kraemer 1987).

Resistance training programmes for children should be

- consented to by parent and child,
- child-orientated and individualised,
- only one part of a total exercise programme,
- closely supervised by an adult,
- competently taught with emphasis on safety and quality,
- balanced, incorporating all the major muscle groups,
- designed to include only light loads, typically 8 to 10 repeats of any one exercise, and
- increased by only a small amount at a time (5 to 10 percent).

Leg raises

- easy upper-body raises for the back muscles (from lying on front, upper body lifted slowly with control, hips and legs remaining stationary), and
- easy push-ups for the chest and arm muscles (against a wall or on all fours on a mat).

Upper-body raises

Push-ups

The focus should be on quality, not quantity. It is not necessary for children to count repeats before they understand the purpose of exercises and can perform them safely with good technique. Controlled lifting and lowering should be emphasised and children should perform no more than 10 to 12 repeats of each exercise before resting. Children who are unfamiliar with the exercises should start by performing 4 to 6 repeats of each exercise and progress over time to 10 to 12 repeats. It is important that they are taught to stretch out the muscles which they have been working.

Correct Ways of Lifting and Carrying

Back pain is one of the most common medical complaints in Britain. It is often the result of many years of incorrect lifting and carrying techniques. Teaching children to lift and carry safely is an important lifeskill.

The recommended way to lift and carry is to

- get close to the object being lifted,
- keep a wide, solid base with feet apart and firmly on the ground,
- use the large leg muscles rather than the back muscles,
- tighten the tummy muscles,
- keep the back straight when lifting or lowering,

- hold the object close to the body, and
- get assistance if the object is very heavy (National Back Pain Association 1990; YMCA of the USA 1994).

It is helpful for storage areas to be organised with a well-planned layout. This improves access to equipment, ensures increased safety in moving equipment and reduces the need for excessive and prolonged carrying of large items of equipment.

Children's understanding and skill in correct lifting, carrying and lowering can be assessed by watching them put out and put away equipment during lessons. Children can be taught the correct method of lifting and lowering when they are asked to move mats, benches or small sections of gymnastic equipment such as a box top. Additional information about back care could be delivered in classroom lessons, perhaps within a topic such as 'Looking After Your Body' or 'Back Care'. For example, many children carry large bags over one shoulder, which can place stress on the spine. They should be encouraged to wear rucksacks over both shoulders to balance the load.

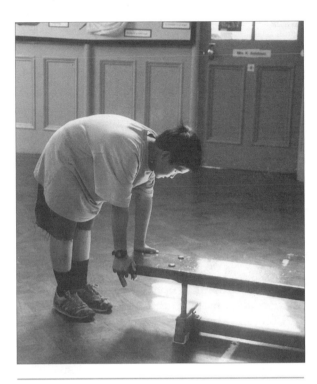

Incorrect lifting

Correct lifting

Incorrect carrying

Correct carrying

Children should understand that

- the back is made up of many small bones called the spine,
- the spine is covered with large muscles,
- the spine is important because it holds the body up and gives the body shape,
- the spine is involved in standing, sitting, bending, reaching, twisting and turning movements,
- it is important that the back and tummy muscles surrounding the spine are strong, and
- the spine needs to be well looked after because it has to support the body as long as you live.

Special Exercise Situations

Some children have specific exercise needs because of health conditions such as asthma or obesity.

What Exercise Is Suitable for Overweight Children?

Overweightness can be described as an excess of body weight relative to height, and obesity is a surplus of fat (Buskirk 1993). Childhood obesity is a common condition in Britain and North America (Armstrong and Welsman 1994; Bar-Or 1994). It is a public health concern because we know that a high percentage of overweight children become overweight or obese adults (Lefebre 1994). Overweight and obese children are likely to suffer from health conditions such as increased blood pressure and raised blood sugar levels, reduced capability to perform everyday tasks, and social and psychological problems such as low self-esteem.

The Role of Exercise in Weight Control

Overweightness and obesity are usually the result of an imbalance in energy expenditure, with energy intake regularly exceeding energy expenditure during routine activity and exercise. An important strategy in dealing with it is to increase physical activity. Children who are overweight or obese should be encouraged to decrease their energy intake gradually by eating fewer high-calorie foods and to increase their energy output progressively by being more active.

Obese children do not necessarily eat more than their peers, nor are they always less active. Indeed, as a result of their increased body mass, obese individuals generally use more energy for a given weight-bearing activity (such as walking) than non-obese individuals. However, obese children tend to spend more time in sedentary activities. Reducing inactivity (such as TV watching) may be as important as increasing activity.

The Best Activity for Weight Control

The best exercise for body fat and weight reduction is activity that generates a large energy expenditure but minimises the risk of injury, discomfort and muscle soreness (American College of Sports Medicine 1983; Buskirk 1993; Malina and Bouchard 1991). The emphasis should be on increasing the frequency and duration of the exercise sessions, so that the child is active more often and for longer. The exercise should be relatively easy to perform, to permit longer duration and encourage increased frequency. Walking, playing, swimming and water exercise, fun games and activities, and being active at home and school are very acceptable forms of exercise for overweight and obese children.

Some children mistakenly believe one must perform very energetic exercise (such as fast running) to 'burn fat' and lose weight (Harris 1993, 1994c). This confusion may lead to some children overlooking or abandoning milder exercise as a way of controlling weight.

The Role of the School

The school should provide children with sound advice about eating habits and activity levels. For example, children should be taught that

- energy comes from food and drink,
- a certain amount of energy is essential for vital body functions (such as breathing and digestion),
- drastic changes in eating habits can be harmful to growth and development,
- if energy intake is greater than energy expenditure, the body stores the excess as fat,
- sensible eating habits and an active way of life help to maintain a healthy weight,
- all forms of activity use energy (walking, cycling, playing, dancing),
- it is not necessary to run fast or to be good at games or exercises to use up energy,
- the same total amount of energy is used in running a mile as walking a mile, and
- a half-hour walk uses more energy than a 10-minute jog.

Education and Eating Disorders

Some people are worried that teaching children about weight management may increase the incidence of eating disorders, such as anorexia nervosa and bulimia, among young people. A high proportion of adolescent girls and a smaller proportion of boys are dissatisfied with their body shape and wish to weigh less (Court 1994). They may feel under pressure to present a certain body image. A study of British children aged 9 to 11 found that as many as 61 percent of children worry about their weight, girls significantly more than boys (Almond and Morris 1995). Concerns about body image act as a barrier to participation in exercise for some girls, and a powerful motivator for others (Orme 1991; Sports Council for Wales 1994).

Teaching all children basic facts about weight management should help them adopt a balanced approach, involving sensible eating habits and an active way of life. For example, children should understand that during the normal growth process of early and mid-adolescence, increases in fat mass occur (particularly in girls). They should also understand that being underweight is as much a health concern as being overweight, and that many people diet unnecessarily. Some physical educators consider that 'sensible exercise and eating' should be a central topic for primary schools and that the role of physical activity in weight control can be taught during active lessons (Biddle and Biddle 1989).

Education and Sensible Weight Control

Teachers should not do any more than give advice on a healthy lifestyle to overweight and moderately obese children, because inducing children to lose weight may only set them up for ultimate failure (Court 1994). Restrictive diets, which can adversely affect physical and emotional development and may cause a reduction in physical activity, may not be appropriate for all obese children.

Obesity in childhood and adolescence is very hard to treat (Buskirk 1993; Court 1994). Each child must be treated individually, after assessment of the family situation, and taking account of physical, social, emotional and motivational factors. The most promising strategies for weight control in childhood seem to include

- a diet that is easy to adhere to and promotes growth,
- an appealing physical activity schedule that promotes energy expenditure,
- behaviour modification programmes for children and parents,
- family involvement, and
- nutrition education (Court 1994; Hawks and Richins 1994).

Successful school-based programmes focusing on childhood obesity have involved a combination of reduced calorie diet, increased activity, and behaviour modification (Bar-Or 1994; Buskirk 1993; Court 1994).

Helping Overweight Children to Exercise

It is important to deal sensitively with overweight and overfat children when exercising, to ensure that activity sessions are positive experiences for everyone.

- Treat pupils as individuals, not comparing and contrasting them.
- Encourage a range of physical activities including non-weight-bearing exercises such as swimming, exercise in water, and cycling.

- Encourage low-impact activities such as walking, and provide low-impact alternatives (such as marching) to high-impact exercises (such as jogging).
- Schedule rest periods to allow recovery from activity.
- Ensure correct exercise technique to minimise the risk of injury.
- Permit a choice of exercise clothing that reduces embarrassment.
- Ensure the wearing of supportive footwear during weight-bearing activities and use soft surfaces rather than hard surfaces (such as concrete) where possible.
- Provide differentiated tasks to cater for a wide range of ability, including low-level, easier tasks.
- Be aware of potential problems such as breathing difficulties, movement restriction, oedema (fluid retention resulting in swelling), chafing, excessive sweating, and discomfort during exercise.
- Encourage routine activity around the home and school.
- Where possible, provide opportunities for overweight and obese children to be active in a private rather than a public context.
- Enable obese children to follow an individually designed exercise programme based on their particular needs and capabilities.
- Encourage guidance and support from school, family and friends.
- Always provide positive feedback and constant encouragement (Health Education Authority and Physical Education Association 1991).

Exercise for Children With Asthma

People who have asthma are liable to narrowing of the airways, which makes breathing difficult. This narrowing can be sparked off by a number of factors (such as irritants, allergens, weather changes, viral infections, emotions, and exercise), which differ among individuals and may vary over time.

Incidence of Asthma

Asthma is a common respiratory disorder and it particularly affects children up to 10 years of age, boys more than girls (Morton and Fitch 1993). Between 15 and 25 percent of the school-age population in Britain is believed to have asthma (Balding 1994; Carruthers, Ebbutt and Barnes 1995). The incidence of asthma is increasing, although medication helps to keep the majority of children free of symptoms most of the time (Carruthers, Ebbutt and Barnes 1995).

Effects of Exercise on Children With Asthma

Exercise-induced asthma may occur during or after exercise. The usual symptoms are wheezing, coughing, tightness of the chest, and breathlessness. More than 80 percent of children with asthma experience these symptoms (McGeorge 1990). However, as regular physical activity has specific benefits for children with asthma (such as decreased frequency and severity of attacks, and reduction in medication), over and above the benefits it has for children in general, it is important that they are encouraged to be active and are integrated as fully as possible into PE lessons and sporting activities. Children with asthma should be able to participate in activities alongside their peers, with minimal adaptation.

A child is most likely to suffer exercise-induced asthma when performing continuous aerobic exercise at a relatively moderate intensity for more than six minutes in cold, dry air (when involved in cross-country running, for example).

How to Help Asthmatic Children Exercise

Although it is important to treat each child individually, there are some general recommendations that should be followed during exercise.

- Encourage the use of an inhaler 5 to 10 minutes before exercise.
- Encourage children to have a spare inhaler readily available for use.
- A child arriving for activity with airway constriction should be excused participation for that session.
- Allow a gradual warm-up of at least 10 minutes.
- Permit and encourage intermittent activity—bursts of activity interspersed with reduced intensity exercise.
- Permit lower intensity (easier) activity.
- Encourage swimming—the environmental temperature and humidity of an indoor pool are well tolerated by people with asthma.
- In cold, dry weather conditions, encourage the wearing of a scarf or exercise face mask over the mouth and nose in the open air.
- Encourage breathing through the nose during light exercise—this warms and humidifies the air.

- Do not permit children with asthma to exercise when they have a cold or viral infection.
- Where possible, advise children with severe asthma to avoid exercise during the coldest parts of the day (usually early morning and evening) and in times of high pollution.
- If symptoms occur, ask the child to stop exercising and encourage them to use an inhaler and to rest until recovery is complete.
- In the case of an asthma attack, send for medical help, contact the child's parents, give medicine promptly and correctly, remain calm, encourage slow breathing, and ensure that the child is comfortable (McGeorge 1990; Morton and Fitch 1993).

Many well-known sportspeople have asthma, including the cricketer Ian Botham and the athlete Jackie Joyner-Kersee, and many world championship level performances in almost all sporting events have been recorded by people with asthma (Morton and Fitch 1993). There is nothing to prevent the vast majority of children with mild to moderate asthma participating in a range of physical activities with minimal difficulty, providing that they take appropriate precautions before and during exercise.

A Word About Inhalers

Although you should encourage children with asthma to participate in PE as fully as possible, you must be aware of possible limitations. Children should have free and easy access to their inhalers (Morton and Fitch 1993). It is not wise for schools to keep asthma medication in a central store. A study based on primary schools in England revealed that 17 percent of teachers stored inhalers centrally, 53 percent kept inhalers under their own supervision, and only 31 percent allowed children to keep their own inhalers (Carruthers, Ebbutt and Barnes 1995). The same study demonstrated that teachers who are better informed are more able to help children with asthma lead a normal life.

Key Points

- Children respond to exercise differently than adults.
- Children should follow a balanced programme of developmentally appropriate physical activities.
- Warm-ups and cool-downs are important—they should be fun, active, varied, and relevant to the lesson.
- Good flexibility helps to prevent injury and improve performance.
- A variety of weight-bearing activities will help to improve strength.
- Good back care is important, including recommended lifting, carrying, and lowering techniques.
- Overweight and obese children should be helped to experience positive activity sessions.
- Children with asthma should be encouraged to be as active as possible, taking appropriate precautions before and during exercise.

3 Health-Related Exercise in the National Curriculum

We need to help children to understand what happens to their bodies when they exercise, and why it happens. This understanding will help them to value exercise and to appreciate its place in a healthy and active lifestyle. Health-related exercise (HRE) will give them the knowledge, understanding, physical and behavioural skills, and also the attitudes required to encourage long-term frequent involvement in health-promoting physical activity. School HRE programmes should provide children with a base of positive attitudes, knowledge and skills to carry over into adolescence and young adulthood. Indeed, it has been suggested that:

> The epidemic of lifestyle related diseases is an educational failure, not a medical failure (Bailey 1989, p. 4).

Aspects of HRE

Schools must promote activity, but it is not enough merely to keep children active in PE lessons. Children should learn through their involvement in activity, and need help to understand the 'why' of exercise as well as the 'what'. HRE focuses on what all children can gain from taking part in a wide range of different types of physical activity, rather than on physical competence.

The concept of health promotion (helping people to avoid illness, rather than curing ill people) has come to the fore in recent years. This involves helping people to adopt positive health behaviours such as exercising frequently, eating sensibly, and not smoking. The government recognises the importance of physical activity in improving the quality of people's lives and is in the process of working out strategies for increasing physical activity levels, especially those of children and young people. PE in schools has an important role to play in health promotion, according to the 1992 *Health of the Nation* report:

> The provisions of the PE National Curriculum stress the importance of physical activity and require pupils to show that they recognise its importance and the effect that activity—or the lack of it—can have on the body (Department of Health 1992, p. 62).

However, at present there does not appear to be much systematic teaching of health-related physical activity in primary schools, or suitable provision for it in primary teacher education (Biddle and Biddle 1989). Armstrong and Biddle (1992) believe that all physical educators should promote active lifestyles more explicitly and health-related physical activity must be a central issue in PE.

What Are the Important HRE Messages?

The teaching of HRE aims to encourage and help more children to become more active more of the time. Here are some of the vital messages of HRE:

- Exercise can be enjoyable and fun.
- Exercise is for all.
- Everyone can benefit from exercise.
- Everyone can be good at exercise.
- Exercise is for life.
- Excellence in HRE involves maintaining an active way of life.

What Are the National Curriculum Requirements?

The promotion of an active way of life through effective exercise education is highlighted in the National Curriculum (NC).

1. HRE is a statutory component of the PE programme for all children (Department for Education and the Welsh Office Education Department 1995; National Curriculum Council 1992).
2. HRE is also a component of the cross-curricular theme of health education (National Curriculum Council 1990).

The NC requirements are presented in chapters 5 and 6, where KS 1 and 2 are discussed in more detail (see pages 52 and 69-70). These chapters present interpretations of the HRE statements and end-of-KS descriptions, together with practical lesson examples.

Physical Education General Requirements

In addition to these detailed requirements, the NC specifies general requirements that apply to the teaching of all PE lessons across all key stages. Examples are:

1. Pupils should be taught to
   - be physically active,
   - adopt the best possible posture and appropriate use of the body,
   - engage in activities that develop cardiovascular health, flexibility, muscular strength and endurance,
   - lift, carry, place and use equipment safely, and
   - warm up for and recover from exercise.

2. Thus, teachers of PE should ensure that all lessons
   - are active for all children (with minimal queuing and waiting for turns),
   - include a wide variety of safe exercise activities,
   - develop stamina, strength and suppleness, and
   - provide positive exercise experiences for all children.

3. The NC requires that, by the age of 11, the ability of children to recognise and understand exercise effects and to sustain activity are assessed and reported to parents. The lesson examples in chapters 5 and 6 include workable procedures for assessing progress and achievement in HRE.

The Role of the Primary School Teacher of PE

School PE has tremendous potential for reaching virtually all children through structured physical activity programmes.

Starting at Primary Level

Primary school PE lessons, combined with a health focus in the classroom, may help children acquire knowledge, attitudes and values which will lead them to participate in physical activity on a long-term basis. This role of the primary school has been generally acknowledged:

> Schools and teachers continue to play a critical role in laying the foundations of young people's lifetime involvement in sport and recreation (Sports Council 1993, p. 6).

> In childhood, the school curriculum in PE and other subjects should cover health related exercise and sport so that children acquire skills, interests and hobbies that will last a lifetime (Sports Council and Health Education Authority 1992a, p. 138).

Enjoyable exercise experiences supported by appropriate explanations can help to establish positive attitudes which are vital for long-term participation.

Areas Needing Attention

Although school programmes may be capable of enhancing activity and fitness levels, exercise understanding and attitudes towards activity, it is not clear how well they succeed in doing this (Dishman and Dunn 1988).

A study by the Sports Council (1993) suggests that schools do not always effectively promote physical activity to all children. In primary school playgrounds, boys usually dominate the space playing ball games (where these are allowed) whereas girls play less energetic games in small groups in smaller spaces.

In mixed PE lessons, teachers tend to spend a disproportionate amount of time on boys. Early

socialisation and differences in opportunities outside school probably make boys more physically competent than girls to start with, and this contributes further to the disadvantagement of girls in the area of sport and exercise. Women's participation in sport in adult life is affected by a lack of basic skills and confidence due to inadequate development of these important factors early on (Sports Council 1993).

The primary school teacher can influence future participation through

- the curriculum (providing an effective HRE course),
- extra-curricular opportunities (such as playground activities or clubs), and
- links with home and with other agencies (such as secondary schools or local clubs).

Recent reviews of physical activity and young people (McGeorge, Almond and Hawkins 1995; Sports Council 1995) have made a number of recommendations for the future which affect primary schools.

- Build on the philosophy of 'sport for all' which is a reality amongst the very young.
- Improve the foundation experience of girls and explore ways to extend and maintain their involvement through the teenage years.

- Extend the PE time in schools to a minimum of two hours per week.
- Develop physical activity as a central element of the NC.
- Decrease the emphasis on competitive sports.
- Provide greater in-service training for primary school teachers, nursery and play group leaders.
- Involve ancillary staff, parents, and older children in developing fun activities.
- Promote activity through parents and the community.
- Encourage safe, active transportation for children (walking or cycling to and from school).
- Improve liaison between the various organisations involved in the provision of physical activity for children.

Teaching HRE

The content and style of delivery of HRE lessons are important. Effective delivery is essential in transmitting the philosophy underpinning HRE and in positively affecting young people's attitudes towards involvement in exercise.

Teaching the 'What' and the 'Why'

In the past, teaching children 'what' has been favoured over teaching them 'why'. Traditional teaching methods relied on the assumption that, through activity, children automatically 'pick up' information about the benefits of exercise and can relate this information to their own lifestyles. However, studies have shown that children and teenagers

- are often unaware of the value of exercise,
- do not know the amount of exercise they should be doing,
- are not aware of exercise opportunities in their local area, and
- are generally confused about exercise messages (Harris 1993, 1994b).

It is totally inappropriate to require children to perform 'fitness' exercises without helping them to understand the reasons why (National Association for Sport and Physical Education 1992). The 'why' and the 'what' of exercise should be taught alongside each other so that children develop knowledge, understanding and positive attitudes as well as physical skills and competencies. Skill development and fitness education should come hand in hand.

HRE can pervade and permeate the whole PE programme, but this should not imply that it can be 'caught', rather than 'taught' (Harris and Elbourn 1992a, 1992b, 1992c). The teaching of health-related concepts should not be left to chance.

How Can the Teaching of HRE Be Organised?

There are several ways of organising the teaching of HRE within the curriculum, including

- permeation,
- focused,
- topic, and
- combined methods.

Teachers are in the best position to determine the most effective method of delivering the statutory HRE content. Curriculum leaders in PE are familiar with their own curriculum, colleagues, children and resources and can therefore make appropriate decisions about the approach to be adopted in their own school. The ultimate responsibility of teachers is to deliver the statutory requirements effectively in order to combat the trend towards an uninformed and sedentary nation. Educators advocate a 'whole-school' approach to the teaching of health education and to the promotion of physical activity in order to ensure coherence and continuity for all children (Curriculum Council for Wales 1994). The whole-school approach is described in detail in chapter 4.

Which Is the Most Effective Approach?

Each of the approaches mentioned above has strengths and limitations.

Permeation Approach

Permeation is an integrated approach in which HRE is taught through the PE activity areas (athletics, dance, games, gymnastics, swimming, and outdoor and adventurous activities). An example of this would be to teach KS 1 children to recognise the effects of exercise on their breathing rate during a games lesson (see chapter 5).

Strengths

- HRE knowledge, understanding, and skills can be seen as an integral part of all PE experiences.

- Children learn that all physical activities can contribute toward good health and can become part of an active lifestyle.

Limitations

- HRE knowledge, understanding, and skills may become 'lost' or marginalised amongst other information relating to skills and performance.
- There may be an overload of information for children.
- Much liaison is required to ensure that all children receive similar information through PE lessons delivered by different teachers.
- The approach may be rather piecemeal. Much of the teaching of HRE through the PE activity areas in secondary schools is unstructured (Harris 1994a, 1995) and minimal health-related content is permeated through conventional PE lessons (Curtner-Smith, Chen and Kerr 1995).

Focused Approach

This focused approach involves teaching HRE through specific lessons or units of work within a PE or health education programme. The main focus of these lessons is the learning concept rather than the activity itself. An example of this would be teaching KS 2 children to sustain exercise over appropriate periods of time and to understand the effects of exercise on their bodies during a series of lessons which might include a variety of activities such as skipping, running, and simple exercises (see chapter 6).

Strengths

- HRE is perceived to be more important when it has its own time slot and identity; this helps to raise the value and status of the associated knowledge, understanding, and skills.
- About 75 percent of secondary schools in England teach HRE through focused units, although many of these schools also use other methods such as permeation through the activity areas (Harris 1994a).

Limitations

- HRE may be seen in isolation and not closely linked to PE activities such as athletics, dance, games, gymnastics, outdoor and adventurous activities, and swimming.
- The HRE knowledge, understanding, and skills may be delivered over a long period of time with long gaps in between (one short block of work per year, for example) which may cause problems for cohesion and progression.

- The way the knowledge base is delivered may reduce the activity levels of lessons (such as 'sitting down' lessons with lots of teacher talk).

Topic Approach

The topic approach involves a series of PE activities and classroom lessons following a specific topic or theme. An example would be teaching children to recognise and value the effects of exercise on the body through PE and classroom lessons on a topic such as 'My Body' or 'Being Active'. Topic-based work may incorporate both permeation and focused units.

Strengths

- HRE can be delivered in a more rounded, holistic manner with closer links to other health behaviours such as taking care of oneself and eating well.
- The area can be covered in more depth and closely related to children's personal experiences.
- The amount of time spent engaged in physical activity in PE lessons can be increased if introductory and follow-up work is conducted in the classroom setting.

Limitations

- A topic- or theme-based approach may take more time to plan.
- This approach may be less practically oriented than the others.

Combined Approaches

Any combination of the above approaches is possible. For example, permeation, focused units, and topic work could be incorporated at various times during KS 1 and 2. All of the specific examples stated above could be used in the following way:

KS 1:
  - Permeation through PE (dance, games, gymnastics)
  - Topic (such as 'My Body' or 'Being Active')

KS 2:
  - Permeation through PE (athletics, dance, games, gymnastics, outdoor and adventurous activities, swimming)
  - Focused units (such as Understanding Exercise; Keeping Up With Exercise; Exercise and Me; Being Active)

Strengths. A combined approach can build on the strengths of different approaches and minimise their limitations. It can also ensure that value is placed on HRE and that the area of work is closely linked to all PE experiences and other health behaviours. In secondary schools in England the combined approach is the most common (Harris 1994a), with well over a third of schools teaching HRE through a combination of focused units, some permeation through the PE activity areas, and within other areas of the curriculum (such as Health Education, Lifeskills, or Personal and Social Education).

Limitations. Combined approaches may initially take a lot of time to plan, structure, implement, and co-ordinate within the curriculum.

A Good Example of an Effective Approach

A combined approach, such as the one described here for KS 1 and 2, has a lot to be said for it. In particular, it ensures that links are made with all forms of activity and with other health behaviours.

Permeated or Integrated Elements

During KS 1, within the activity areas of dance, games and gymnastics, children are helped to recognise the range of short-term effects that happen to their bodies during exercise (see chapter 5).

Focused Aspects

During KS 2, some focused practical lessons may help to highlight NC requirements.

- Sustaining energetic activity over appropriate periods of time (over a few weeks, for example, gradually increasing the time spent on activities such as walking, jogging, skipping, swimming and dancing). The Exercise Challenge four-week exercise programme for 9- to 13-year-olds is a suitable and helpful resource (see chapter 4).
- Understanding the short-term effects of exercise on the body (see chapter 6).

Topic- or Theme-Based Component

An approach based on a topic or theme such as 'My Body' or 'Healthy Lifestyles' or 'Staying Healthy' can assist in teaching the following Health Educa-

tion concepts that the NC requires be learned in primary schools:

- People feel better when they take exercise.
- Exercise strengthens bones, muscles and organs and keeps the body supple.
- Exercise uses energy which comes from food and that the body stores excess as fat when energy intake is greater than energy expenditure.

Possible Cross-Curricular Links in HRE Lessons

Many cross-curricular links can be made when planning and delivering HRE lessons. The samples here are for Science, Mathematics and English (Department for Education 1995). Some of these possibilities have also been utilised in the lesson examples presented in chapters 5 and 6.

Science

Several of the science components of the NC may be linked with aspects of HRE. The relevant NC components are given in brackets.

Key Stage 1

At KS 1, teachers should give children opportunities to

- ask questions, such as How? Why? What will happen if...? (Systematic Enquiry),
- use both first-hand experience and simple secondary sources to obtain information (Systematic Enquiry), and
- consider ways in which science is relevant to their personal health (Science in Everyday Life).

Children should be taught

- that thinking about what they expect to happen can be useful when planning what to do,
- to make observations and measurements,
- to make a record of observations and measurements,
- to communicate what happened during their work,
- to make simple comparisons,
- to use results to draw conclusions,
- to indicate whether the evidence they have collected supports any prediction they made,

- to try to explain what they found out, drawing on their knowledge and understanding,
- to describe the movement of familiar things,
- to name the main external parts of the human body, and
- that taking exercise and eating the right types and amount of food help us to keep healthy.

Key Stage 2

At KS 2, children should be given opportunities to

- use both first-hand experience and secondary sources to obtain information, and
- relate their understanding of science to their personal health.

Children should be taught

- a simple model of the structure of the heart and how it acts as a pump,
- how blood circulates in the body through the arteries and veins,
- the effect of exercise and rest on pulse rate,
- that we have skeletons and muscles to support our bodies and to help us to move,
- that forces acting on an object can balance and that when this happens an object at rest stays still, and
- that unbalanced forces can make things speed up, slow down, or change direction.

Mathematics

Several of the mathematics components of the NC may be linked with aspects of HRE. The relevant NC components are given in brackets.

Key Stage 1

Teachers should give children opportunities to understand the language of numbers, properties of shapes and comparatives.
    Children should be taught

- that thinking about what is expected to happen can be useful when planning,
- to describe and discuss shapes and patterns that can be seen or visualised (Shape, Space and Measures: Understanding and Using Patterns and Properties of Shapes), and
- to describe positions, using common words; recognise movements in a straight line (translations and rotations), and combine them in simple ways; copy, continue and make patterns (Shape,

Space and Measures: Understanding and Using Properties of Position and Movement).

Key Stage 2

Teachers should give children opportunities to

- understand and use the language of the properties and movements of shapes (Using and Applying Mathematics: Developing Mathematical Language and Forms of Communication),
- consider a wide range of patterns, including some drawn from different cultural traditions (Shape, Space and Measures), and
- access and collect data through undertaking purposeful enquiries (Handling Data).

Children should be taught to

- choose appropriate standard units of length, mass, capacity and time, and make sensible estimates with them in everyday situations (Shape, Space and Measures: Understanding and Using Measures); and
- interpret tables used in everyday life (Handling Data: Collecting, Representing and Interpreting Data).

English

There are many ways in which the English components of the NC may be linked with aspects of HRE. The relevant NC components are given in brackets.

Key Stage 1

Teachers should give children opportunities to talk for a range of purposes, including

- exploring, developing and clarifying ideas;
- predicting outcomes and discussing possibilities;
- describing events, observations and experiences;
- making simple, clear explanations of choices;
- giving reasons for opinions and actions (Speaking and Listening: Range); and
- writing in response to a variety of stimuli, including stories, poems, classroom activities and personal experience (Writing: Range).

Key Stage 2

Teachers should give children opportunities to talk for a range of purposes, including those already mentioned for KS 1, and also

- planning, predicting, and investigating;
- sharing ideas, insights and opinions; and
- reporting and describing events and observations (Speaking and Listening: Range).

Key Points

- All PE lessons should be active, safe, and positive.
- HRE is a statutory component of the NC.
- Past experience suggests that HRE is not 'caught' and therefore should be 'taught'.
- HRE can be taught through permeation, focused units, topic work, or a combination of approaches.
- A combined approach maximises strengths and minimises limitations of other methods.
- Many cross-curricular links are possible between HRE and the NC core subjects.

4 *Whole-School Approach*

Children may have only two or three PE lessons a week, so additional activity sessions will have to be at break times or lunch hours, after school, in the evenings or at weekends. Teachers and parents can help to provide children with additional opportunities to be active. A whole-school approach to promoting a way of life in which physical activity is valued and integrated can help to ensure that

- all children receive consistent and coherent health messages,
- children are helped to relate these messages to their everyday life situations,
- physical activity is valued alongside other health behaviours,
- all staff are promoting physical activity to every child, and
- opportunities to be active are made available to all, irrespective of age, gender, ethnicity, impairment, and physical competence.

Schools are in an ideal position to have a positive influence on children's health behaviour, because they provide

- a captive audience of children for most of the year,
- a range of relevant professionals (teachers or nurses, for example),
- physical activity facilities all year round,
- established lines of communication with parents and guardians, and
- an environment conducive to multidisciplinary programmes (Bar-Or 1990, 1994).

Primary schools are in a particularly favourable position to promote physical activity, because

- young children are curious about their own bodies and receptive to health information,

- the primary school teacher oversees the whole development of the child and can more easily integrate health information, and
- there is often close liaison with the home (Sleap 1990).

It is important to instil the values and concepts of active living in the school environment (Campbell 1994). For primary schools in particular:

The whole school's approach to healthy activity can lay the basis for a positive attitude towards active recreation (Sports Council 1993, p. 18).

The aim is not just a healthy school but a healthy community and a healthy environment. Schools need to work in partnership with parents and local groups to develop the notion of an 'active community' in which physical activity is valued and encouraged. A co-operative and collaborative approach is particularly important given the trend towards reduced PE time in schools (Harris 1994c) and a more automated and sedentary way of life.

Whole-school approaches include

- school award schemes such as the Health Promoting School and the Active School;
- award schemes for children, such as the Exercise Challenge, the Fitness Challenge and the Skipping Award Scheme; and
- a range of activity promotion events and practical ideas which focus on participation in health-promoting physical activity.

The Health Promoting School

Health Promoting School schemes aim to assist schools in providing effective health education and a healthy environment for the school community (Health Promotion Authority for Wales 1992; Northern Ireland Curriculum Council 1994; Wessex Institute of Public Health Medicine and Hampshire County Council Education Department 1993). Schemes are supported by resources and staff training. Schools can work towards and apply for a Health Promoting School or Healthy School Award. Schools that demonstrate achievement or progress towards a specific number of Health Promoting School targets are eligible for awards.

A Health Promoting School promotes and provides a healthy lifestyle for everyone who teaches, learns and works in it by

- working towards NC guidelines for health education,
- offering a wide range of physical activities accessible to all,
- encouraging a smoke-free environment,
- offering children and staff healthy food choices,
- encouraging children to take responsibility for their own health, and
- ensuring that policies reflect the school as part of a wider community.

Schools may be required to demonstrate that

- HRE is integrated with other aspects of health,
- curricular and extended curricular opportunities are available for all children, and
- the school is involved in the promotion of opportunities for active lifestyles in the local community.

Health Promoting School schemes are especially valuable for HRE because they highlight its place in the curriculum and they help the school community to value the place of physical activity and exercise within a balanced healthy lifestyle.

Information about Health Promoting or Healthy School Award schemes can be obtained from the address on page 137.

The Active School

Active Schools is a national promotion that encourages schools to work out an action plan to increase the participation of children in physical activity, within and beyond school (Almond and McGeorge 1995).

In recent years physical education has tended to emphasise participation in physical activity beyond PE lesson times. The overall aim of an Active Schools policy is to make physical activity a better experience for more young people more of the time, and so increase participation rates. Related objectives include forming action plans to increase physical activity amongst children, staff and parents, and the initiation of healthy alliances which facilitate the promotion of HRE for young people. Key principles underpinning the Active Schools philosophy are that all individuals should be valued and respected and that there should be sensitivity towards and tolerance of individual differences, needs and interests.

Active Schools should promote activity that is fun, which leads to achievement, that brings recognition and promotes self-worth.

There are many ways in which levels of physical activity could be increased in schools. Some of these are

- increasing the activity levels of PE lessons (e.g., by reducing team sizes),
- ensuring differentiation in PE lessons so that all children can succeed,
- ensuring that competitive experiences are positive and fair,
- individualising exercise experiences,
- designing a Sports Day which involves every child (through personal challenges or group activities and games),
- monitoring fitness and activity levels in and out of school (using diaries, for example),
- organising participation challenges such as the '1000 Club' (see pages 45-46),

- organising festivals on specific activities (such as dance, games, skipping),
- introducing 'taster' sessions for children to try out new activities,
- introducing participation award schemes (such as gaining points for activity),
- encouraging a wide variety of playground activities (with a 'card box' of ideas and/or an equipment box, or through playground markings),
- organising open-access weekend activities (such as 'Saturday Morning' sessions), and
- organising special activity promotions (such as a Jump Rope for Heart 'Jump Off').

Schools interested in the Active Schools promotion and the Active School Award scheme should contact the Exercise and Health Group at the address given on page 137.

The Exercise Challenge

The Exercise Challenge is a scheme which encourages young people to be more active. It helps deliver the HRE requirements of the NC, provides an opportunity to reward children for positive health

behaviour, and helps promote links between teacher, child and parent. The scheme is detailed in a teacher's manual and is accompanied by booklets (McGeorge 1993). Children complete an exercise profile in which they consider their current activity levels and take part in simple fitness monitoring procedures such as a recovery pulse rate after exercise, modified curl-ups and push-ups, and a 'sit and reach' flexibility measurement. The fitness monitoring procedures are designed to be non-threatening, informative and individualised, and the emphasis is on current activity levels rather than fitness scores.

After the initial profile, 9- to 13-year-old children embark on a four-week Exercise Challenge which involves them following a prescribed exercise programme. Each exercise programme contains a balance of cardiovascular activity (stamina), muscular strength and endurance exercises (strength), and flexibility exercises (suppleness). The level of the programme in terms of frequency (how often), intensity (how hard) and duration (how long) is determined by the baseline activity level of the individual child. For example, a child who currently exercises less than once a week would follow an easier exercise programme than one who exercises three times a week or more. The exercise programmes are designed so that the frequency and duration of the exercise gradually progress over the four weeks. There is a wide choice of cardiovascular activities (such as brisk walking, skipping, swimming, cycling or dancing) and different levels of exercises to develop muscular strength and endurance, and flexibility.

Children participate in some of the activities during PE lessons and are encouraged to complete the rest of the programme in their own time. They record their exercise in a diary which is signed by an adult (teacher, parent, guardian) at the end of each week.

Children compare their activity levels at the end of the four weeks with their activity levels before starting the Exercise Challenge, and repeat the fitness monitoring procedures. They are asked to make a simple evaluation of personal differences between the 'before' and 'after' recordings and are encouraged to consider the benefits of an active lifestyle. Everyone who completes the Exercise Challenge is rewarded with a certificate. The certificate is intended to reward positive exercise behaviour (completing the exercise programme) rather than any changes in fitness monitoring results.

The major benefits of the Exercise Challenge as an award scheme are that

- it is attainable by all children,
- it links with the NC, and
- it rewards effort and behaviour, not performance and natural talent.

Information about the Exercise Challenge can also be obtained from the Exercise and Health Group (see page 137).

The Fitness Challenge

The Fitness Challenge is an incentive scheme for children aged between 4 and 13 years and is aimed at encouraging participation in any form of physical activity (University of Hull 1994a, 1994b). The scheme is simple to organise and can be run by teachers, lunch-time supervisors, Cub and Brownie leaders, parents, coaches, youth organisers and sports leaders. Children can also enter the scheme themselves, taking part individually or with friends.

The scheme is based on participation, with no performance criteria, and it offers success to any

child, regardless of gender, disability or skill level. Children record activity periods of at least 15 minutes. There must be no more than one activity period per day and they cannot include PE lessons. All forms of physical activity can be included such as games playing, dancing, roller skating and skateboarding. Bronze, silver and gold awards are achieved for 12, 24 and 36 activity periods respectively. Medals and certificates are available for children who complete the award.

Information about the Fitness Challenge can be obtained from Children's World Fitness Challenge at the address given on page 137.

Skipping Award Scheme

The Skipping Award Scheme is designed to be an alternative to many award schemes which are predominantly performance-orientated. The award scheme was designed around principles of inclusion, participation, progression, balance, choice and challenge (Harris and Almond 1991). It develops five main areas: skill, endurance, responsibility, sharing and creativity. The scheme incorporates a concern for safety factors and includes such tasks as finding the correct length for a rope, putting a rope away safely, and warming up and cooling down. These tasks focus on developing individual responsibility. Because rope jumping is a high-impact activity which can put stress on the joints, some tasks incorporate low-impact ('twirling') activities to encourage participants to mix impacts within their skipping routines.

Details of the Skipping Award Scheme

The Skipping Award Scheme is open to children over the age of five. The scheme has six levels which each comprise ten tasks (two from each of the five areas of development). Each level is achieved by attaining eight out of the ten tasks (with at least one from each of the five areas of development). The scheme can be entered at any appropriate level and the tasks can be attained in any order within a level.

Level 1

1. Perform 10 continuous forward skips.
2. Perform 10 continuous backward skips.
3. Skip continuously for 30 seconds.

4. Keep the rope moving continuously for 30 seconds without jumping it.
5. Show how to check the correct length of a skipping rope.
6. Show how to tie up and put away a skipping rope safely.
7. Perform 10 continuous skips facing a partner in the same rope.
8. Perform 10 skips side by side with a partner in the same rope.
9. Design a hopping and jumping sequence over a rope laid on the floor.
10. Turn a rope in two different ways without jumping it.

Level 2

1. Perform three different skills using two foot bounces.
2. Perform three different skills using one foot bounces.
3. Skip continuously for one minute.
4. Keep the rope moving continuously for one minute without jumping it.
5. Warm up for skipping without using a rope.
6. Explain two important skipping safety points.
7. Show a short skipping sequence to an adult.
8. Describe to someone the effects on the body of skipping.
9. Find a way of jumping the rope and travelling forwards at the same time.
10. Find a way of jumping the rope and travelling backwards at the same time.

Level 3

1. Perform a short sequence showing four different footwork skills.
2. Perform a short sequence showing four different armwork skills.
3. Skip continuously for two minutes.
4. Keep the rope moving continuously for two minutes without jumping it.
5. Warm up for skipping making use of a rope.
6. Show one important stretch that should be performed after skipping.
7. Teach someone else a skipping skill.
8. With a partner holding the other end of your rope, find a way of jumping in and out of the rope.
9. Find two different ways of jumping the rope and travelling sideways at the same time.
10. Design an individual skipping routine showing changes of speed.

Level 4

1. Change from forward skipping to backward skipping, and from backward skipping to forward skipping.
2. Perform four different footwork skills with the rope turning backwards.
3. Skip continuously for three minutes.
4. Keep the rope moving continuously for three minutes without jumping it.
5. Cool down after skipping making use of a rope.
6. Keep a diary over three weeks and record your skipping sessions.
7. Arrange for a small group to skip together at the same time.
8. Teach a small group two different skills.
9. Find three different ways of skipping with a partner in the same rope.
10. Design an individual skipping routine showing a variety of rotations.

Level 5

1. Perform two different skills which combine footwork and armwork.
2. Perform a short sequence combining armwork and rotations.

3. Skip continuously for four minutes.
4. Keep the rope moving continuously for four minutes without jumping it.
5. Lead a short warm-up with a small group.
6. Lead a short cool-down with a small group.
7. Show a small group two different ways of working with one long rope.
8. Teach two people the skills needed for double dutch rope turning.
9. Design a short group sequence that involves a line formation.
10. Design a 'two in one' rope routine which shows footwork and rotations.

Level 6

1. Perform a short sequence which includes footwork, armwork and rotations.
2. Perform a short sequence which includes travelling, twirling and rotations.
3. Skip continuously for five minutes.
4. Keep the rope moving continuously for five minutes without jumping it.
5. Design and perform a skipping session which includes a warm-up and a cool-down.
6. Design and follow a six-week skipping programme and record your progress.

7. Teach a small group the skills needed for double dutch skipping.
8. Teach another person to perform 'Chinese Wheel'.
9. Design a formation routine for a small group that includes a line and a circle.
10. Design and perform a routine with a partner that involves footwork, armwork and rotations.

The Skipping Award Scheme has been successfully piloted in a small number of schools in England but has yet to be formally launched. Further information can be obtained from the Exercise and Health Group (address on page 137).

Youth Sport Trust

The Youth Sport Trust is a registered charity that has been established to work in partnership with the Sports Councils, with support from the National Coaching Foundation and Loughborough University and from private sector funding. Its mission is to develop and implement quality sport programmes for young people aged 4 to 18 years. These programmes are co-ordinated nationally and delivered locally. The aims of the Trust include the desire for all children

- to have fun and success in sport,
- to experience positive competition, and
- to form a sound foundation for lifelong physical activity.

The Youth Sport Trust and the Sports Council deliver four programmes in schools and communities. These programmes, TOP Play, TOP Sport, Champion Coaching and TOP Club, are part of a wider national junior sports initiative being managed and co-ordinated by the Sports Council. Details can be obtained from the Youth Sport Trust at the address on page 137.

TOP Play

TOP Play involves core skills and fun games for 4- to 9-year-olds. It is based on essential sporting skills such as throwing and catching, jumping and hopping, and hitting and stopping. The programme offers national training and specially designed equipment for use in schools and playcentres. Resources are available in the form of user-friendly laminated cards focusing on specific sporting skills, such as rolling and kicking. Each card clearly illustrates a specific task involving the skill and acts as a prompt for children to use by themselves or with appropriate guidance.

TOP Sport

TOP Sport introduces sport and games to 7- to 11-year-olds, as a progression of the sporting activities from TOP Play. The programme provides resources that are complementary to the delivery of the curriculum and after-school sport, and training for volunteers to assist with delivery. Again there are laminated cards, this time focusing on specific sports, such as rugby, tennis and netball. Each card displays a game activity with playing instructions, essential safety points and appropriate modifications. The cards can be used by children independently or with teacher guidance. Fit for TOP Sport is a component of the TOP Sport programme and aims to meet the health and fitness needs of children.

Champion Coaching

Champion Coaching focuses on improving the performance of 11- to 14-year-olds. The mission of the programme is to promote quality assured youth sport coaching for performance motivated children within a co-ordinated community structure. Champion Coaching has helped over 100 local authorities to offer programmes in 15 sports to 11- to 14-year-olds. The programme offers training for coaches and youth sport managers, and provides resources to help inform and build a sustainable community structure for young people and their coaches.

TOP Club

TOP Club helps clubs to build a future in sport for children of all ages. The programme provides expertise, in selected sports, to help clubs plan for the positive involvement of young people, and to develop a junior club strategy which can be implemented across the country in co-operation with local authorities. TOP Club offers financial assistance, planning expertise, coaching development and strong links with national governing bodies of sport.

Promotional Events

Promotional activities are good starting points for increasing awareness of healthy lifestyles and for making contacts with people and groups in the local community—parents, businesses and services, for example. Many schools have organised events with a health focus, ranging from assemblies and open evenings to weekend and whole-week activities.

Titles used for these events have included:

Get Up and Go

Jump for Joy

Fun 'n' Fitness

Come Alive

Exercise for Life

An event like this might involve

- all school staff, including secretarial and ancillary staff;
- parents and governors;
- media coverage;
- the use of a variety of subject lessons to focus on the theme;
- planned activities for breaks, lunch times, after school, evenings and weekends;
- workshops run by outside groups;
- talks and presentations from outside groups;
- appearances by celebrities or special guests;
- displays (of food, exercise equipment or local organisations);
- health breaks and lunch times (such as selling fruit at the tuck shop);
- planning special activities (such as parachute drop, ramble, barn-dance, fun run); and
- designing special event T-shirts, posters and leaflets.

A wide range of physical activities could be included in promotional events: aerobics, archery, barn-dancing, bike riding, country dancing, dance class, disco dancing, fitness testing, Frisbee throwing, fun circuit, fun run, golf, mixed games, novelty races, obstacle course, orienteering, relaxation, roller disco, skipping, water polo, windsurfing and yoga, to name just a few!

Presentations and display subjects which might be included in promotional events are active holidays, beauty care, cooking with fruits, coping with stress, using exercise equipment, fitness for life, good health and healthy eating.

Schools who have hosted health promotion events know from experience the tremendous amount of liaison work, collaboration, energy and creativity they require. However, published accounts of these events have unanimously emphasised the beneficial impact of a focused event on a school community (Health Education Council and Physical Education Authority 1986; Richardson 1989). One-off promotions have their limitations, but they can be especially valuable in terms of raising awareness of a particular theme which can then be developed over an extended period of time through curriculum courses and extra-curricular provision.

Jump Rope for Heart Programme

Jump Rope for Heart is a sponsored skipping programme organised by the British Heart Foundation (BHF) to encourage children to take part in exercise that is healthy and fun. The funds raised are used for research into heart disease, which is Britain's main cause of premature death and disability. In order to become involved in the programme, a school, youth club or group registers with the BHF's Jump Rope for Heart scheme. They are sent a free skipping chest which includes numerous skipping ropes, an organisation booklet, sponsor forms, a skipping book, music cassette, teacher's notes (including suggested lesson plans), and an organiser's T-shirt.

Once children have learned and practised skipping skills, a sponsored 'Jump Off' can be organised. The 'Jump Off' involves teams of up to six members, and the teams skip for a maximum of three hours with each person skipping for about two minutes at a time. More than one team member can be jumping at once to reduce the total time. The participants seek donations, or can be sponsored for parts of, or the whole, event. The group may retain 25 percent of the money raised from the 'Jump Off', the remaining 75 percent going to the BHF.

Anyone interested in registering for a 'Jump Off' fund-raising event should contact Jump Rope for Heart at the address on page 137.

Activity Promotion Ideas

A wide variety of activity promotion ideas have been successful in different schools (Elbourn and Harris 1990).

1000 Club

The 1000 Club is a promotional activity over a set period of time (such as 12 weeks) which aims to encourage children to take part regularly in a range of exercise activities. Every child taking part is given a log sheet (see page 46) and asked to write down the type and amount of exercise that they complete during the period of the event. Points are awarded according to the duration of the exercise, and bonus points can be gained by taking part in exercise at the weekend, or by encouraging others to exercise at the same time.

Sample of 1000 Club Details

Record below any jogging, swimming, cycling, skipping, brisk walking, running, dancing or aerobics you do during the school term and ask an adult (parent, teacher or guardian) to sign the sheet to confirm you did it.

1000 Club certificates will be issued to everyone who logs 1000 points of activity in one school term. All achievements will be recorded in your personal school profiles.

The points system is simple—you get 1 point for every minute of activity that you do, such as

- 5 points for 5 minutes of activity,
- 10 points for 10 minutes of activity,
- 30 points for 30 minutes of activity, and so on.

You can also get bonus points! Here's how:

Add

- 5 points if you do the activity on a Saturday or a Sunday,
- 10 points if you take someone else (such as a friend) with you,
- 20 points if you introduce someone to the 1000 Club, and
- *double* your points for the activity if you can persuade any adult relative (such as your mum, dad, aunt, uncle, grandparent) to join in with you.

Jogalong

The aim of the Jogalong is to encourage as many people as possible to take part in regular exercise that promotes cardiovascular health. The Jogalong can be held over a period of weeks and the Jogalong charts (see page 47) can be handed in at appropriate times during that period. At the end of the Jogalong, awards or certificates of achievement can be presented to individuals or groups who have done well.

Sample of Jogalong Details

1. Go for a jog on the school field—either by yourself or with a friend who is willing to jog with you.

2. Try to jog without stopping—this means running at a steady pace so that the exercise feels fairly energetic but not exhausting.

3. When you have completed your jog, cool down by walking round for two or three minutes and stretching out your lower leg (calf) muscles.

4. Record your jogging on your Jogalong chart.

Advice

1. Do not jog immediately after you have eaten a meal.

2. Change into suitable clothing for jogging and remember to bring a towel for a wash or shower afterwards.

3. Do not jog if you have a cold or are feeling unwell.

4. Try and pace yourself so that the jog is steady and comfortable. If you are jogging with someone else, you should be able to jog and chat at the same time.

5. Try to build up your own jogging time by adding on another minute each time you go for a jog. Try to build up to a 15- or 20-minute jog.

Skipalong

The Skipalong is organised in a similar way to the Jogalong. Making a gym or hall facility available for use during break and lunch times (with the provision of ropes and motivating music) can contribute to its success.

Sample of Skipalong Details

1. Skip for a period of time—either by yourself, or with a friend who is willing to do some skipping at the same time as you.

2. Try to skip at a steady pace so that the exercise feels fairly energetic but not exhausting. If you get tangled up, get yourself sorted out and carry on skipping.

1 000 Club					
Name:					
Date	**Activity**	**Time taken (in minutes) = points**	**Any bonus points? What for?**	**Total points**	**Authorised by**
e.g., 1/5/95	Cycling	15	+ 15 (took brother)	30	P. Perkins
				TOTAL =	

Jogalong			
Name:		Class/tutor group:	
Date	Person I jogged with	Amount of time I jogged	How I felt
e.g., 15/7/95	Rob Parker	15 minutes	Okay
		TOTAL =	

3. When you have finished skipping, cool down by walking round for two or three minutes and stretching out your lower leg (calf) muscles.

4. Record your skipping on your Skipalong chart (see page 49).

Advice

1. Do not skip immediately after you have eaten a meal.

2. Change into suitable clothing for skipping and remember to bring a towel for a wash or shower afterwards. Supportive footwear is essential for skipping. Do not skip in bare feet.

3. Do not skip if you have a cold or are feeling unwell.

4. Try and pace yourself so that the skipping is steady and comfortable.

5. Try to build up your own skipping time by adding on another minute each time you skip. Try to build up to 5 to 10 minutes of steady continuous skipping. Keep your feet low to the ground when skipping and place your heels down as frequently as possible.

Jump Rope Challenges

The aim of the 1000 Skips Challenge is for children to try to skip 1000 times during a set period of time (such as one or several school days). Each child receives a skipping challenge sheet which they complete during this period. Each child is challenged to complete 1000 skips with other people. This could involve 100 skips with 10 different partners, 50 skips with 20 different partners, or any other permutation. Pupils are responsible for asking their skipping partners to sign their skipping challenge sheets (see page 50). A central scoreboard in the school could be used to record how many children have met the challenge or, alternatively could maintain a running total of the number of skips completed by the whole school. It may be possible to set the challenge 'Skip to a Million!' over a suitable period of time.

Key Points

- A whole-school approach ensures coherent, consistent health messages.
- School award schemes can assist in effective health education delivery.
- Activity award schemes for children promote active lifestyles by rewarding positive health behaviour.
- Inclusive activity award schemes reward participation, not performance.
- Activity promotion events can increase awareness amongst a community and initiate future longer-term developments.

Skipalong			
Name:		**Class/tutor group:**	
Date	**Person I skipped with**	**Amount of time I skipped**	**How I felt**
e.g., 4/2/95	Ray Elbourn	5 minutes	A bit tired
		TOTAL =	

1 000 Skips Challenge/Skip to a Million!		
Name:		**Class/tutor group:**
Date	**Signature of partner**	**Number of skips**
e.g., 25/5/95	*Pat Maunsell*	100
		TOTAL =

5 Key Stage 1 Lesson Examples

The example lesson plans in this chapter illustrate how the HRE requirements can be taught through dance, games and gymnastics at KS 1. Learning focuses on selected HRE requirements which are taught through the activity-specific Programme of Study. Cross-curricular links with subjects such as mathematics and science are identified (Department for Education 1995) and the resulting content of each lesson is a 'rich' educational mixture. However, HRE should remain the focus throughout each lesson, and assessment tasks should highlight the selected HRE learning outcomes.

When planning schemes of work, various decisions need to be made which focus on

- inclusion of the material in one lesson or over a series of lessons showing progression of learning,
- prior learning within the specific activity area,
- modification of tasks to enable children to progress at their own level,
- opportunities for reinforcing HRE learning outcomes in future lessons and in other activity areas, and
- progression of the warm-up and cool-down activities over a series of lessons (for example, a particular warm-up could be repeated over several lessons).

The example lessons aim to fulfil the relevant general requirements for PE. They are predominantly active, and focus on learning through practical involvement. Preparatory and follow-up ideas for the classroom are included at the end of each lesson plan. Relevant background knowledge is also included. We have suggested ideas for differentiation which should help children to learn at their own level and pace.

Each lesson makes use of simple equipment, and suggestions for suitable working areas. The lesson plans provide sufficient material for approximately 30 minutes of working time, but they can be adapted for shorter or longer lessons. Appropriate stretches for inclusion in the warm-up and cool-down of each lesson are described in table 2.3 on page 17.

Assessment

Assessment should be an integral part of the teaching and learning process. It should be easy to administer, time efficient, and focused on relevant aspects of learning. Through assessment, you can determine the learning needs of individual children and the success of the teaching and learning strategies you have used. In planning lessons, it is necessary to decide what to assess, and how to organise and implement assessment, with large numbers of children in a practical teaching and learning context (Harris and Elbourn 1992c; National Curriculum Council 1992). Assessment should be ongoing, and should use a wide range of teaching and learning styles. A variety of assessment opportunities are included in the example lesson plans, to provide guidance for delivery of suitable tasks which focus on specific HRE learning outcomes. Some of them make use of follow-up work which might be carried out in a classroom setting.

KEY STAGE 1 HRE IN THE NC

KS 1: HRE REQUIREMENTS IN THE NC

Throughout KS 1 children should be taught to

- recognise and describe the changes that happen to their bodies during exercise, and
- recognise the short-term effects of exercise on the body (Department for Education and Welsh Office Education Department 1995).

At the end of KS 1, they should be able to demonstrate this understanding.

As a result of health education at this stage children should

- know that people feel better when they take regular exercise, and
- know that exercise uses energy which comes from food (National Curriculum Council 1990).

INTERPRETING HRE IN THE NC FOR PE AT KS 1

During KS 1, children should learn to recognise and describe these specific changes that happen to their bodies during exercise:

- An increase in rate and depth of breathing
- An increase in heart rate
- A flushed appearance
- An increase in body temperature
- Moist and sticky skin
- A number of feelings about activity (tired, lively, energetic, fun, boring, etc.)
- Involvement of large muscle groups (such as leg and arm muscles)

Pupils should be taught to warm up for exercise by

- preparing their bodies in a gradual manner,
- performing exercises which move their bones and warm their muscles,
- performing activities which make them feel ready for further activity, but not 'puffed out', and
- performing whole-body stretches.

Pupils should be taught to recover from exercise by

- helping their bodies to recover in a gradual manner,
- performing cool-down activities which make them feel 'OK' and not out of breath, and
- performing whole-body stretches (Harris and Elbourn 1992a, 1992b).

Key Stage 1: Teaching HRE Through Dance

LEARNING OUTCOMES

HRE: To enable children to explore the changes that occur to their pulse rates as a result of participating in dance activities

Dance Programme of Study: To help children to develop control, co-ordination, balance, poise and elevation in the basic actions of travelling, jumping, turning, gesture and stillness.

Cross-Curricular Links

Mathematics: To enable children to describe positions using common words, recognise movements in straight and curvy lines, copy, continue and make patterns, and understand the language of comparatives.

EQUIPMENT

- One hoop per child
- Background music (optional)
- Heart beat and heart rate scale

Starting the Lesson

Say to the children:

Do you know where your heart is? It is inside your chest underneath your ribs. It is not quite in the middle of your chest, but is to the left hand side.

Place your hand on your rib cage and slightly to the left hand side. Can you feel your heart? What is it doing?

Where are you on the heart beat scale? Where are you on the heart rate scale?

Heart beat scale

Tap tap	Boom boom!

Heart rate scale

Very slow	Very fast

Our hearts always beat even when we are asleep.

Today we are going to explore what happens to our hearts when we take part in some dance activities.

Warm-Up

This warm-up focuses on interpreting descriptions of positions in space through movement.

1. Ask each child to collect a hoop and to place it on the floor.

2. Ask them to travel to the following locations in relation to the hoop:
   - Inside the hoop
   - Next to the hoop
   - In front of the hoop
   - Behind the hoop
   - Around the hoop
   - Around someone else's hoop
   - Far away from the hoop
   - Close to the hoop

Tell them that they do not need to stay in contact with the hoop. Encourage them to use a variety of different ways of travelling to these new locations (sliding, stepping, skipping or turning, for example) and to work at a steady speed. As far as possible, activity should be continuous.

3. When children are familiar with the travelling activity, introduce mobility exercises by asking them to trace large controlled circles with body parts (hands, arms or legs). When they are sufficiently warmed up, they can perform whole-body stretches. Each stretch should be held still for 6 to 10 seconds.

Activity 1: Exploring Travelling Actions in Straight and Curvy Pathways

1. Ask the children to travel to another hoop in the room in a straight pathway (without turning any corners on the way or crossing other hoops). When they have reached this hoop, ask them to travel towards another hoop, once again using a straight pathway. Challenge them to travel in a variety of ways (such as jumping and turning) and ask them to perform their straight journeys at different speeds.

2. Now ask the children to travel amongst the hoops using curvy pathways (winding around the hoops with no sharp corners or straight lines). Ask them to perform their curvy journey at different speeds.

3. Say the following to the children:

Place your hand on your heart. What can you feel?

Where are you on the heart rate scale?

Describe the speed of your heart beat—is it beating faster, slower, or the same as before?

Where are you on the heart beat scale?

Describe how your heart beat feels—is it strong and thumping, or light and gentle, or somewhere in between?

Activity 2: Building Up a Vocabulary and Performing Movement Patterns

Children need to develop a vocabulary of useful words that describe positions in space. In this example the stimulus of 'a journey in a strange place' is used.

1. The children work in pairs. One partner holds, suspends or supports one or two hoops in any position at a medium or low height. The other partner embarks on a 'journey' through the room. Encourage them to use a variety of methods of travelling (such

as jumping, stepping, sliding or turning). Challenge them to travel through, around, under, over, towards and away from the hoops. After a short time the partners should swop roles. Ask them to describe some of the ways in which they negotiated the hoops (through, under, over, in, out, around or in between).

2. After storing the hoops away, the children are asked to design 'a journey in a strange place'. They brainstorm what might be found in their 'strange place' (trees, caves, tunnels, ladders, bridges, staircases or holes) and discuss ways in which they might have to travel around, over, through, along, behind and across these objects. Give them time to explore movement ideas for their own journey. Suitable background music can be helpful.

3. During this exploratory work, challenge the children to include straight and curvy pathways and to use a variety of ways of travelling, turning and jumping.

4. Ask them to select their favourite moves (such as negotiating two or three obstacles) and to practise this part of their journey, making sure that they know the route well. The journey should have an interesting starting and finishing position that they can hold still.

5. Again ask them the questions about heart rate and heart beat in Activity 1 (page 55).

6. Now ask the children to lead a partner through their journey. When the journey is completed, the partner who is following describes to the leader where it took them (for example, 'we crept around in a small circle and then skipped straight to the other side of the room and then used a wiggly pathway to jump and step back to the start'). The partners then swop roles and repeat the exercise.

Cool-Down

The children repeat their own journey once more, but this time all the movements are much slower. When they have reached the end of their journey, lead them in performing some whole-body stretches. The stretches should be held for 10 to 12 seconds.

Conclusion and Assessment Opportunities

Yet again, ask the children the questions about heart rate and heart beat in Activity 1 on page 55.

To assess the effect of the lesson, you can use the heart rate and heart beat scales as prompt sheets. The children can ask their partner the answers to some questions, for example:

What happened to the speed of your heart beat when you were dancing?

What happened to the strength of your heart beat when you were dancing?

You can listen to individual children or to the pair discussions to assess their understanding of the effects of exercise on the heart rate.

Preparatory and Follow-Up Ideas

1. The idea of a continuum can be introduced in the classroom. It can be linked to other areas of the curriculum. For example:
   - number line (mathematics),
   - dark and light (science),
   - loud and silent (science and music), and
   - slow and fast (music).

Alternative learning contexts are useful in familiarising children with the heart rate and heart beat scales. For example, in music, they can use percussion instruments played at different speeds and with varying dynamics.

2. Children can illustrate their created journey by drawing or painting line patterns representing the route they took.

3. Using the idea of the journey as a stimulus, the children can create their own musical piece for simple instruments (triangle, shakers, suspended cymbal and wood block). You might record the completed compositions and use them as musical stimuli for dance lessons.

Differentiation

The tasks included in the lesson are open-ended and allow children to participate at their own level.

Key Stage 1: Teaching HRE Through Games

LEARNING OUTCOMES

HRE: To enable children to explore the changes that occur to their breathing rate as a result of participating in games activities.

Games Programme of Study: To help children to develop and practise a variety of ways of sending, receiving and travelling with a ball.

Cross-Curricular Links

Science: Experimental and Investigative Science Programme of Study—To enable children to think about what is expected to happen, make observations, and communicate what happened during their work.

Mathematics: Using and Applying Mathematics Programme of Study—To enable children to understand the language of comparatives.

EQUIPMENT

- One ball (size 4 or smaller) per pair of children or one ball per child
- Two marker cones, skittles or cones for each pair of children
- One breathing rate chart (see figure on page 59) per child
- Coloured pencils or crayons

Starting the Lesson

Tell the children what the lesson is about:

When we exercise, lots of different changes happen to our bodies.

Today, we are going to explore what happens to our breathing when we exercise.

After we have warmed up, we are going to play some games using a ball.

What do you think will happen to your breathing when you play the games?

Will it stay the same as it is now or will it change?

Wait for some answers before going on.

How can you find out whether your breathing has changed?

If you place one hand on your tummy and one on your chest, you can feel your own breathing. Count each time your chest rises and falls as one breath. Try to breathe as normally as you can while feeling your breathing rate.

Give the children time to do this before going on.

Draw lines on your chart to link those words which best describe your breathing now with the box that says 'before I exercise'.

Draw lines on your chart in a different colour to show what you think will happen to your breathing when you are playing games. Link the describing words with the box that says 'when I exercise'.

Warm-Up

1. Children work in pairs, and the children in each pair are numbered 1 and 2. Number 1 skips anywhere in the space. Number 2 follows their partner as closely as possible. On the teacher's instruction, they change over so number 2 becomes the leader.

2. The children lift their knees high and clap their hands under each knee as they lift it.

3. Ask them to repeat the pair work, but this time the leaders travel holding a ball in their hands. On the teacher's instruction, number 1 gives the ball to number 2 who becomes the leader.

4. The children stand back-to-back in their pairs and pass the ball over their heads and beneath their legs, keeping their legs slightly bent.

5. Ask them to repeat the pair work with the balls again.

6. In each pair, number 1 throws the ball into the air and number 2 tries to catch it after it has bounced once. Ask them to repeat this task several times, swopping roles each time.

7. Lead the children in performing a whole-body stretch, which should be held still for 6 to 10 seconds.

8. Repeat item 3.

9. Again lead them in performing a whole-body stretch, holding still for 6 to 10 seconds.

Standing whole-body stretches

Activity 1: Carrying and Sending a Ball

1. Children work in pairs, and are numbered 1 and 2 in each pair. Each pair has one ball and one cone or skittle.

2. Each pair stand facing each other, a short distance apart. There should be enough space between the pairs to allow the children to travel around their partners.

3. Number 1 runs around their partner and back to their place, holding a ball. When they have returned to their place, they roll their ball accurately along the ground to their number 2 who traps the ball with their feet or hands and then picks it up. Number 2 then runs around number 1, and repeats the activity. You may want to demonstrate the game with one of the children, taking on the role of number 1 yourself.

4. Use the following teaching points to encourage the children to *pass* the ball accurately:

Bend your knees.

Look where you want to send the ball.

Let your hands swing back and let them follow the direction of the ball after you let it go.

5. Use the following teaching points to encourage the children to *receive* the ball effectively:

Watch the ball carefully.

Position yourself behind the ball.

Get your hands or feet ready to trap the ball.

Activity 2: Dribbling and Sending a Ball

1. Explain the development of the game using one of the following methods:
   - Stop the whole class and explain and demonstrate.
   - Teach one pair the new activity and use them to demonstrate to the whole group.
   - Visit each pair or small groups of pairs in turn and develop their game while the rest of the class performs the previous activity.

2. Number 1 dribbles the ball using their feet or hands around their partner and back to their place. Number 1 then passes the ball accurately to their partner using their feet or their hands and number 2 traps the ball with their feet or hands, and the game continues. The pass between partners must travel along the ground.

3. Encourage the children using the following teaching points:

Keep the ball close to your foot/hand all the time when you are dribbling.

Keep the ball under control all the time when you are dribbling.

When passing using your feet, use the inside of your foot to strike the ball.

Swing the foot/arm backwards to prepare for your pass.

Look where you want to send the ball.

When you have passed the ball, let your foot/hand follow the ball in the direction you want to send it.

Keep your eyes on the ball when receiving.

Be prepared to move quickly to position yourself behind the ball.

Get your hands or feet ready to trap the ball.

When this activity is over, ask the children:

Put one hand on your chest and one on your tummy—can you feel your breathing?

What has happened to your breathing as a result of playing the games?

Can you think of words to describe your breathing now?

Activity 3: Shooting and Dribbling a Ball

1. Each pair needs two cones. These cones are positioned as a mini-goal about 4 to 5 metres away from a starting line. The cones should be about 1.5 to 2.5 metres apart. Adjust this distance for different children within the group as necessary.

2. Number 1 kicks the ball towards the mini-goal. Number 2 stands behind the goal and traps the ball with their feet or hands after it has crossed the goal line. Number 2 dribbles the ball back to the starting line while number 1 jogs to the mini-goal and stands behind the line ready to receive their partner's shot.

3. Every successful shot at goal (one that passes between the goal posts) scores one point.

Developments

1. Challenge children to score as many points as possible in one minute, working as a pair.

2. After a short rest and a discussion with their partner, challenge them to improve their score.

At the end of this activity, again ask the children the questions about breathing rate on page 61, then add:

After the lesson you will be recording the findings on a chart.

Activity 4: Scoring and Dribbling Challenge

This is played in exactly the same way as the previous activity, except that the goal is moved one pace further away from the starting line after both players have performed successful shots and traps at the shorter distance.

1. If a shot is not accurate and/or the ball is not trapped successfully by both players, the goal remains in the same position.

2. Point out that if their goal has moved further away from the starting line, this is an indication of their accurate shooting and good trapping skills.

Cool-Down

1. Ask the children to walk or skip and collect one piece of equipment each (cone or ball). Repeat this until all the equipment has been collected in.

2. The children perform one whole-body stretch for 10 to 12 seconds, copying you.

3. Ask them to perform another whole-body stretch to finish the lesson.

Conclusion and Assessment Opportunities

Ask the children to refer to the breathing rate charts they drew earlier:

Draw lines on your chart to describe your breathing while you were playing games. Look at the line you drew earlier. Are the lines the same? If they are, it means that you were able to guess what would happen to your breathing when you played games.

Choose three words to describe how your breathing changed during exercise. For example:

When I was playing games, my breathing was _____ and_____ and _____ than it was before exercise.

While the children are actively involved in activities 1 to 4, circulate among them, asking individual children simple questions to assess how well they recognise the effects of exercise on the breathing rate. At the same time, you can give help and advice on the performance of the task and skill development.

Preparatory and Follow-Up Ideas

- The breathing rate chart can be introduced in the classroom before the games lesson.
- The investigation of breathing rate can form part of a science project which focuses on planning experimental work, and obtaining and considering evidence.
- Follow-up work involving discussion of the breathing rate chart can also take place in the classroom.

Differentiation

Pupils are given a choice of ways to trap and travel with the ball (with the hands or the feet, for example). They can choose which method is most suitable for them. You can offer advice if children have chosen a skill level that is either too demanding or insufficiently challenging.

In activities 3 and 4, the goal can be made wider or narrower for different pairs according to their skill level.

Key Stage 1: Teaching HRE Through Gymnastics

LEARNING OUTCOMES

HRE: To enable children to recognise that large muscles are working during gymnastic activities and to explore different feelings that people experience when exercising.

Health Education: To help children to recognise that people feel better when they take regular exercise.

Gymnastics Programme of Study: To enable children to explore balancing and travelling on hands and feet and to link a series of these actions on the floor.

Cross-Curricular Links

Science: Life and Living Processes Programme of Study—To enable children to name the external parts of their bodies.

EQUIPMENT

• One gymnastic mat for each pair of children

Starting the Lesson

Engage the children in a dialogue about muscles:

Where are your muscles? (Underneath the skin.) There are muscles almost everywhere in your body—arms, legs, tummy, back.

What do muscles help you to do? (To move—to lift, to carry, to run, to climb stairs, to play games.)

Are your muscles working when you are not moving? You might not know the answer to this question at the moment, and we will think about this again later in the lesson.

Today we are going to explore when our muscles are working in gymnastics.

Warm-Up

This warm-up will also help to revise the names of the external parts of the body.

1. Space the mats in the working area. Ask children to move in between them and to explore as many different ways as possible of travelling on their feet.

2. Stop the children. Ask them to take their body weight on to two hands and one foot using the mat that is nearest to them. (More than one child can use each mat.) Explain that this position of control and stillness is called a balance.

3. When the children have relaxed from the balance, lead a mobility exercise (arm circles and upper-body twists, for example).

4. Ask the children to resume their travelling actions between the mats, then do another balance and a different mobility exercise. You should suggest the different body

parts for each balance (one hand and two feet, two feet only, bottom and one hand, one shin and one hand, one foot only, etc.).

5. When the children are sufficiently warm, substitute a whole-body stretch performed on a mat for the balance and mobility exercises. Pupils continue to perform travelling actions between each of the selected stretches. Each stretch should be held for 6 to 10 seconds.

6. Ask the children to travel between the mats as before. Now present problem-solving challenges relating to the number and combination of body parts required for each balance. For example, the challenge of three feet and three hands will require either three children on one mat each balancing on one hand and one foot, or two children on the mat, one balancing on both feet and both hands, and the other on one hand and one foot. Pupils can be asked to assess whether their peers have answered the task accurately, and to help them to make adjustments where necessary.

Activity 1: To Explore a Variety of Ways of Travelling on Hands and Feet

The children explore different ways of travelling on hands and feet in response to tasks suggested by the teacher. For example:

Find ways of travelling on hands and feet with your back facing the floor.

Find ways of travelling on hands and feet in which both hands and both feet are moving at the same time.

Place your hands on the floor, jump your feet into the air, and bring your feet down in a different place.

Travel on two hands and one foot, or two feet and one hand.

Travel on hands and feet with hands and feet close together or far apart.

Say to the children:

Show me the travelling action where you placed your hands on the floor, jumped your feet off the floor, and brought your feet down in another position.

When your feet are in the air, which muscles are working? (The muscles in the arms are working hard because they are supporting your body.)

How do your muscles feel when they are working hard? You may feel them tiring and they may feel warm and tight.

Are your muscles working harder now than before the gymnastics lesson?

Let's stand up. Which muscles are supporting your body now? (The legs, back and tummy muscles.)

Are our leg muscles working even when we are just standing still? (Yes, but they are not working as hard as when we are running or jumping.)

Activity 2: Taking Weight on Different Body Parts and Holding Balances

The children explore different ways of taking their weight on a variety of body parts and holding balances, in response to tasks you suggest. For example:

Find a balance on three parts of the body, for example, bottom and two hands, or shoulders and two feet.

Find a balance on two matching body parts, for example, two hands or two feet.

Find a balance on two different body parts, for example, hip and hand, or one foot and one hand.

Find a balance in which you are upside down.

Find a balance on one body part only.

The following teaching points can assist their performance:

Make sure that your muscles are tight in order to help you to balance without wobbling.

What is happening to the other parts of the body which are not supporting weight?

Can these parts help you to make an interesting body shape?

Try to concentrate while you are balancing and to move into your balance in a slow and controlled way.

Activity 3: Linking Balances With Travelling on Hands and Feet

1. Ask the children to choose two balances they can perform well, and to practise them to make sure that they can hold the balances still.

2. Ask them to perform one balance on their own mat and then travel to another mat using hands and feet only. Organise the movement of children from one mat to another to make sure that children are distributed evenly between the mats. Once they have

established which mat they are travelling to, they can decide which route they are going to take and which travelling actions to use.

3. When children arrive at the next mat, they perform their second balance.

4. Give them time to practise their sequence and ask them to hold each stretch as still as possible so that their choice of supporting body parts is clear.

5. Organise the children so that one can watch another perform the chosen sequence. After the performance, the teacher asks the following questions to all the children:

Did anyone see a balance on one/two/three body part(s)? Which one/two/three body part(s) did the person balance on?

Did anyone see a way of balancing that did not involve hands or feet? What body part(s) was the person balancing on?

6. Ask the children to swop roles and perform the sequence again. Then ask these questions again.

Cool-Down

Pupils travel between the mats using skipping and walking activities. Call out a description of a stretch (such as long and tall, or curled) and ask them to perform an appropriate whole-body stretch on the nearest mat. Each stretch is held for 10 to 12 seconds.

Conclusion and Assessment Opportunities

Ask the children the following questions:

Which parts of your body have you moved during this gymnastics lesson?

Are there any parts of your body you have not moved?

Muscles have to work to make your body parts move. How hard have your muscles been working during this lesson?

Do our muscles work when we are not moving? (Yes, in our balances, the muscles are working to keep our body where we want it to be. If the muscles did not hold our bones up, our bodies would collapse in a heap on the floor!)

Think through the activities that you do during the day (such as climbing the stairs, walking, carrying, lifting, twisting, bending). What do you think is happening to your muscles when you do these activities? (They are working hard.)

If our muscles are not used to working hard, everyday activities like climbing the stairs and walking to school are likely to make us feel tired. How do you think we will feel when doing energetic activities? (Worn out, fed up, tired.)

If we use our muscles regularly by doing exercises such as gymnastics, playing games, dancing, or skipping, our muscles will get used to working hard and everyday actions will feel easier.

How do you think we will feel when doing energetic activities? (OK, lively, happy.)

We can work our muscles by exercising and we can feel good when we are active.

To assess the effect of the lesson, circulate during activity 3 and ask children individual questions about which muscles they are working when they perform the movements included in their sequence.

Preparatory and Follow-Up Ideas

The names of the external body parts can be introduced in a classroom setting. The gymnastics lesson will reinforce this learning and help children to learn the names of areas of the body they may not already know, such as the forearms and shins.

Pupils can observe members of their family to see what physical activities they perform (such as lifting, carrying, digging, sweeping, bending, sawing, climbing). They can ask the person how the activity makes them feel and observe whether they needed to sit and rest after doing it. They could also ask whether the person does any exercise such as jogging, swimming, playing games or attending exercise classes. The children's observations can be shared verbally or as written 'news'.

Differentiation

The tasks included in the lesson are open-ended, so children of all abilities should be able to take part in the tasks at their own level.

6 *Key Stage 2 Lesson Examples*

This chapter is organised in a similar way to chapter 5. It includes example lesson plans for teaching HRE through athletics, games, and outdoor and adventurous activities at KS 2. The comments at the beginning of that chapter about lesson planning and assessment apply equally here.

KEY STAGE 2 HRE IN THE NC

KS 2: HRE REQUIREMENTS IN THE NC

Throughout KS 2, children should be taught

- to sustain energetic activity over appropriate periods of time in a range of physical activities, and
- to understand the short-term effects of exercise on the body (Department for Education and the Welsh Office Education Department 1995).

At the end of KS 2, children should be able to demonstrate the skills and knowledge listed above.

In terms of health education at this stage, children should know that

- exercise strengthens bones, muscles and organs and keeps the body supple, and
- the body stores excess energy as fat if energy intake is greater than expenditure (National Curriculum Council 1990).

INTERPRETING HRE IN THE NC FOR PE AT KS 2

During KS 2, children should learn what happens during exercise:

- Large muscles in the body, such as the legs, are working.
- Muscles need a supply of oxygen to keep working.
- The heart rate increases to pump oxygen to the working muscles.
- The rate and depth of breathing increase to provide more oxygen to the working muscles.
- The appearance can become flushed because blood vessels become wider and closer to the surface of the skin.
- The temperature increases because the muscles produce energy as heat when they are working.
- The skin can become moist and sticky because the body sweats when it is very warm to cool down and avoid overheating.
- People's feelings vary about the types and amount of exercise in which they are involved.

Children should also be encouraged to sustain energetic activity over appropriate periods of time by learning to be aware of

- their current activity levels,
- how moderate to vigorous activity feels, and
- different ways of being moderately to vigorously active, such as skipping, jogging and cycling.

They should

- be moving towards about 30–60 minutes daily of moderate to vigorous physical activity involving up to three or more activity sessions per day, with rest periods as necessary; and
- select moderate to vigorous physical activities that they would enjoy participating in enough to reap health benefits (Corbin, Pangrazi and Welk 1994).

With respect to warming up and cooling down, children should understand the following points:

- Preparing the body gradually to start exercising is comfortable (similar to changing up through car or bike gears).
- Joints (where ends of bones meet) have different actions. Gently moving them helps the bones move more freely.
- Activities that gradually increase the heart rate allow more oxygen to reach the working muscles.
- Muscles move bones, and stretching helps to lengthen muscles safely and prevents them from being torn or pulled.
- Stretches should be held still and should only be performed when muscles are warm.

Children should be able to perform and recognise

- mobility (loosening) exercises which move bones,
- pulse-raising actions which increase gradually in intensity, and
- stretches both for the whole body and for parts of the body.

Children should understand that

- preparing the body gradually to stop exercising is comfortable (similar to changing down through car or bike gears),
- cool-down activities should make them feel 'OK' and not out of breath, and
- the muscles that have been used during exercise need to be stretched to minimise unnecessary stiffness or soreness.

Children should be able to perform

- pulse-lowering actions which decrease gradually in intensity, and
- stretches for the whole body and parts of the body, such as the back of the lower leg, front of the upper leg or the back (Harris and Elbourn 1992a, 1992b).

Key Stage 2: Teaching HRE Through Athletics

LEARNING OUTCOMES

HRE: To raise the children's awareness that they should be moving towards 30 minutes or more of moderate to vigorous intensity exercise per day, which can include activities such as running.

Health Education: To enable children to understand that exercise strengthens the heart.

Athletics Programme of Study: To enable children to develop and refine basic pacing techniques in running over long distances.

Cross-Curricular Links

Mathematics: Number Programme of Study—To help children to use multiplication to solve simple calculations without using calculators.

EQUIPMENT

- Four stacker/marker cones per pupil. (Bean bags, small plastic flag markers or tennis balls can substitute for marker cones.)
- 'How Does the Exercise Feel' chart (table 6.1)
- One stopwatch
- One whistle

TABLE 6.1   'How Does the Exercise Feel' Scale
How does the exercise feel?
1   Very very easy
2   Very easy
3   Easy
4   OK
5   Fairly hard
6   Hard
7   Very hard
8   Very very hard
9   Exhausting
10   Maximum

Starting the Lesson

Talk to the children about activity and exercise:

There are lots of ways of exercising and being active—how many can you think of? (Cycling, skating, swimming, dance, gymnastics, playing games, skipping, brisk walking.)

Why is it important for people to take part in exercise activities frequently? (People will feel better when they take regular and frequent exercise. Some children might also be aware that exercise will help to improve the health of their heart and other muscles.)

How much exercise do we need to do at any one time to improve our health? (Any exercise is better than none, but we should try to gradually increase the time we spend exercising.)

Today we are going to explore running as a way of increasing our own activity levels and to find out how we can gradually increase the amount of time that we can continue running at a steady pace.

Warm-Up

1. Two cones are set out as markers and are placed about 15 to 30 metres apart. Alternatively, two lines approximately the same distance apart can be used.

2. Ask the children to jog together from one cone (or line) to the other at a pace that feels 'very very easy'. Use the 'How Does the Exercise Feel?' chart (table 6.1) to help the children work at an appropriate intensity. Jog with the group and, using a stopwatch, time the group's journey and inform them of this time. At this 'very very easy' intensity the children should probably all be travelling at a similar pace. Help the children to determine an appropriate pace by encouraging everyone to jog together.

3. Ask the children to mobilise their shoulders by performing large controlled arm circles as they walk back to the starting cone or line.

4. Ask the children to repeat the journey between the cones, taking exactly the same time as they did to perform the first journey. Suggest that they pace themselves accurately according to how the exercise feels. Help the group to judge the accuracy of the pacing by calling out the time at the halfway point and when the target time is reached.

5. At the end of the second journey, ask the children to mobilise the upper and lower spine by performing upper-body twists and side bends. These exercises should be performed with control.

6. Ask the children to choose a slightly shorter target time in which the whole group will be able to jog between the cones comfortably. Again you can assist pacing by calling out the time at the halfway point or by calling out the seconds as they pass.

7. At the end of the third journey, the children mobilise their hips in a controlled manner (using knee lifts and hip circles, for example).

8. The time challenge is repeated two or three more times. Each time the children are invited to increase the challenge by reducing the target time and to pace themselves, with or without cues from you. During this part of the warm-up, the children can choose their own personal target times. Remind them that warm-up activities should feel fairly energetic but should still leave them feeling 'OK'.

9. When children are sufficiently warm, lead them in stretches for the back of the lower leg (calf), the front of the upper leg (quadriceps) and the back of upper leg (hamstring). Each stretch should be held still for 6 to 10 seconds.

Activity 1: Making Personal Decisions About Appropriate Exercise Intensity

The aim is to build up running time to five minutes. Challenge the children to choose their own target time for running quickly between the cones. Every pupil sets their own challenge, and you call out the seconds as the group is running. Repeat this two or three times, challenging the children to set faster, slower or the same targets for each journey. After each journey, ask the children to consider how the exercise felt. Linking their own personal speed with their perceived rate of exertion may help the children to pace themselves more accurately.

Now discuss the activity with the group:

We have now been working on running activities for a few minutes. We have been stopping and starting during that time, which has given us time to get our breath back. We are now going to build up to running for five minutes without stopping. Can you remember why building up our exercise time is important? (When we run our heart works harder. The heart is a muscle and when we work a muscle over a period of time it becomes stronger.)

Why is it important to have a strong heart? (Because it is a very important pump. It pumps the blood around the body and the blood carries food and oxygen to our muscles where energy is made.)

If we can keep going when we exercise, our heart will become stronger and it will be able to do its pumping job more easily.

What pace do you think you will choose when running for five minutes without stopping? Will you start at a pace that feels 'very very hard'? Why not? What pace will you choose? How will that pace feel? Will everyone in the class choose the same pace? (No, because some people are not so used to running as others and any exercise feels easier if you are used to it.)

The speed that you travel is not important, because we are all going to exercise for the same amount of time. However, we should all feel as if we are working 'fairly hard' or 'hard'.

What will happen to our bodies when we are working this hard? (We will be breathing harder, we will feel warm, and our hearts will be working fairly hard, but we should not feel exhausted.)

Activity 2: Two-Cone Return-Run Challenge

Again the aim is to build up running time to five minutes.

1. The children each have two cones. They place one cone to mark their starting point and then run with the other cone in a straight line away from the starting point. Ask them to run at a pace that feels 'fairly hard' or 'hard'. Tell them to stop on the whistle and to place their cone on the ground.

2. After 10 seconds, blow the whistle, tell the children the amount of time they have run, and then challenge them to run back at the same pace to reach their starting point in exactly 10 seconds.

3. Ask the children to work out how many seconds it will take to run, at their chosen pace, out to their cone and back to their starting point. Children attempt to pace themselves to complete the two journeys in 20 seconds.

Activity 3: Three- and Four-Cone Return-Run Challenge

Again, the aim is to build up running time to five minutes.

1. Ask children to measure the distance between their cones by counting the number of paces or by using a metre wheel. Then ask them to place a third cone the same distance away from the second cone. Ask the children to calculate how many seconds it will take them to run to this third cone and back to their starting point. They then attempt to pace themselves over this distance, which should take a total of 40 seconds to complete. You can help them by calling out the seconds regularly, say every 10 seconds.

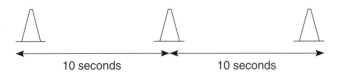

2. Now ask the children to place a fourth cone the same distance away from the third cone, and work out how many seconds it will take to run to the fourth cone and back to their starting point. They should attempt to pace themselves over this distance, which should take a total of 60 seconds to complete. Again you can help them by calling out the seconds. If enough stopwatches are available, children could time a partner.

Discuss the activity with the children:

During the last activity, for how many minutes did you run? (One minute.)

How many journeys between the nearest and the furthest cone did you complete in one minute? (Two.)

In a moment we are going to try to keep running for five minutes. We will be running for five times as long. To calculate any of the sums about our journey, we need to multiply by five.

How many journeys between the nearest and the furthest cone will you complete in five minutes? (Ten.)

Some of you may be finding the pace that you have set feels harder than you thought. If you do not think that you can keep going for five minutes at this pace, slow down. It is better to keep going at a slower pace than to stop completely.

If you decide to travel more slowly to make the exercise feel slightly easier, what can you do with your furthest cone so that you complete the ten journeys in exactly five minutes? (The furthest cone can be moved slightly closer to the third cone.)

If you decide to travel more quickly to make the exercise feel slightly harder, what can you do with your furthest cone so that you complete the ten journeys in exactly five minutes? (The furthest cone can be moved slightly further away from the third cone.)

Activity 4: Five-Minute Return-Run Challenge

The aim is to complete a five-minute run. The children make any necessary adjustments to their cones before attempting to complete five minutes of continuous running at their chosen pace. Again, help them by calling out the minutes. Remind them that they should have run to the furthest marker cone and back every full minute and have reached one of their end marker cones every half minute.

Cool-Down

The children walk to collect their cones. When they have done this, lead them in specific stretches for the back of the lower leg (calf), the front of the upper leg (quadriceps) and the back of upper leg (hamstring). These stretches are held still for 10 to 12 seconds.

Conclusion and Assessment Opportunities

Ask the children how they feel after running:

How do you feel now that you have completed five minutes of jogging?

How do you think the jogging will feel if you complete five minutes regularly (such as every other day)? (It should start to feel easier.)

If jogging for five minutes starts to feel too easy, what can you do? (Increase the amount of time you jog, perhaps to six or seven minutes.)

Calf stretches

Children may also suggest that they could jog more quickly to increase the intensity of the exercise. They can do this if they like, but remind them that they must be able to keep going for at least five minutes.

You have opportunities to ask children, on an individual basis, any of the questions included in the lesson plan.

Preparatory and Follow-Up Ideas

Jogging Challenges

Challenge the children to complete three five-minute sessions of jogging in the next week. Let them discuss where it is possible for them to jog (such as in the school playground, on the school field, along paths or tracks, in public parks and play areas). They should also discuss when it might be possible to jog and whether they might go with a friend or a member of their family. Ensure that children are mindful of safety in the plans they make.

During the following week, you might make provision for them to use an outdoor or suitable indoor area at break and lunch times for this purpose.

After each jogging session, children can record how the exercise feels (such as a bit tired, 'OK', worn out).

At the end of the week, the class can assess how many people are starting to find that the jogging feels easier. They can aim to increase the length of time they exercise during the following week. Some children might be finding the jogging difficult or unappealing, and these children should be encouraged to try different exercises such as brisk walking, swimming or cycling in the following weeks.

Exercise Scales

Children can design their own 'How Does the Exercise Feel' scale. This can provide cross-curricular links with English (Speaking and Listening Programme of Study).

They can use their scales to assess how other exercise activities feel. This work might take place in another PE lesson, or as part of an investigative project undertaken within another subject area such as science. Through such work, children can develop an understanding that exercise activities which are less familiar feel harder to do at first. In future work they can also explore whether these activities feel easier when they are more familiar.

Table 6.1 is an example of a 'perceived rate of exertion' chart which can help children to determine whether they are working at an appropriate exercise intensity. For example, if they are aiming to improve their heart health by increasing the duration of a particular exercise activity, they need to work at a steady pace and the exercise should feel 'OK' or 'fairly hard' (they should be huffing and puffing, but not either struggling for breath or feeling unaffected by the exertion).

- Exercise which feels 'very very hard' or 'exhausting' is unlikely to be sustainable for more than short periods of time.
- Exercise that feels 'very easy' or 'very very easy' is unlikely to be working the heart, lungs and muscles at a sufficiently high intensity to gain cardiovascular health benefits.

Differentiation

Using the perceived rate of exertion ('How Does the Exercise Feel' scale) encourages children to work at their own level. Any overweight or obese children who are having difficulties can be encouraged to walk throughout the activity at a pace which feels comfortable and sustainable for them.

Key Stage 2: Teaching HRE Through Games

LEARNING OUTCOMES

HRE: To enable children to evaluate games as a means of being moderately to vigorously active and to reinforce understanding concerning the effects of exercise on the body.

Health Education: To enable children to understand that playing games can strengthen the bones, muscles and the heart.

Games Programme of Study: To enable children to understand how to create goal-scoring opportunities as an attacking player, through participation in small-sided games.

Cross-Curricular Links

Science: Experimental and Investigative Science Programme of Study (Obtaining Evidence)—To teach children to use simple equipment to make careful observations and measurements, and to use the results of observations to draw and explain conclusions.

EQUIPMENT

- One traffic cone or marker cone per game
- Bibs or bands (different colours)
- Four hoops per game
- One size 4 or 5 ball per pair of children
- One stopwatch or watch with second hand
- One whistle (optional)

Starting the Lesson

Ask the children the questions about exercise on page 72.

Any exercise is better than none, but we should try to build up gradually to exercising for about 30 minutes every day. This can be three or more times a day for about ten minutes each session. Today we will explore how we can increase our activity levels and strengthen our bones, muscles and heart, by playing games.

Warm-Up

1. In pairs, the children jog in the working space and pass the ball between them using their hands. They indicate their readiness to receive the ball by showing their partner the palms of their hands.

2. Stop the children at intervals and demonstrate a mobility exercise. All children perform the mobility exercises with their partner before they go on travelling with the ball. Suitable activities that can be used are presented in table 6.2.

3. When all of the appropriate joints have been mobilised, give each pair two cones to make a small goal anywhere in the playing area. Ask them to travel around the area and to pass the ball to each other through all of the goals. The partner without the ball decides which goal they will go to next. Activity should be continuous.

4. Stop the activity and call out the location of a muscle (such as the groin, the front of the thigh or the chest).

5. The children perform the appropriate stretch for this muscle, which should be held for 6 to 10 seconds. The stretches can be alternated with travelling and passing activities in pairs, to keep the body temperature raised.

6. Organise the children into groups of six and ask each group to make a comment about changes that occur in one of the following during the lesson:
   - Breathing
   - Heart rate
   - Temperature
   - Appearance

Groups discuss simple ways in which they might monitor changes that occur during games playing. More than one group can focus on each aspect. This work reinforces pre-

TABLE 6.2 KS 2: Mobility Exercises for Games Warm-Up	
Mobility activity	**Joints Mobilised**
10 chest or overhead passes with a partner.	Shoulders, elbows, wrists
Standing back-to-back, pass the ball 10 times between the legs (keeping legs bent) and overhead.	Spine, shoulders, elbows, wrists
Standing back-to-back, pass the ball by twisting the waist to one side and then the other.	Upper spine, shoulders, elbows, wrists
Bounce the ball under alternate legs while partner jogs and touches four sidelines (or other relevant landmarks). Swop roles.	Knees, hips, elbows, wrists
Pass the ball around the waist, around the head and between the legs in a continuous sequence while partner jogs and touches four sidelines (or other relevant landmarks).	Hips, shoulders, elbows, wrists

vious investigations focusing on the changes that happen to the body during exercise (see Teaching About the Effects of Exercise on the Body—A Focused Lesson, p. 96).

Activity 1: Creating Scoring Opportunities in a Four-Goal/Three-Defender Game

1. Set up the playing area as illustrated in the figure below. Organise each group of six into two teams of three players, with bibs or bands to distinguish the different teams. The game is a throwing and catching game played with a size 4 or 5 ball.

2. One of the teams is the attacking team and the other is the defending team. The object of the game is for the attacking team to score points by placing the ball in any one of the four hoops. Members of the attacking team cannot run when in possession of the ball. No member of either team is permitted to stand in the hoops.

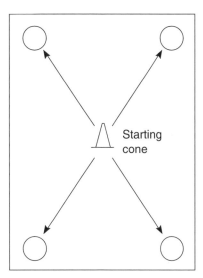

3. The game starts with the attacking team passing the ball from a starting cone placed centrally in the playing area. The defending team aim to intercept the ball. If a defender gains possession of the ball, they put the ball down on the ground and leave it. An attacking team player can pick the ball up and run with it back to the starting cone.

4. When the ball is sent out of court by an attacking player, it is returned straight to the starting cone. If the ball is sent out of play by a defending player, the attacking team throw the ball into the area from the point where the ball went out. The attacking and defending teams change roles after a timed period.

When both teams have played in attacking and defending roles, discuss the game with the children:

How easy is it to score in this four-goal game? (Quite easy because there are only three defenders and four goals and so one goal is always undefended.)

What plan did you use as attacking players? (Move towards the undefended goal. If it becomes defended, quickly switch to attack another undefended goal.)

What is an 'ideal' scoring opportunity? (If an attacking player who is in possession of the ball is close to an undefended goal.)

Activity 2: Creating Scoring Opportunities in a Two-Goal/Three-Defender Game

The playing area remains the same size as before, but there are goals in only two of the corners and the starting cone is now at the centre of the widest sideline (see figure below). The rules for playing remain the same as the first game, with teams taking turns to attack and defend for a set period of time (one to three minutes, for example).

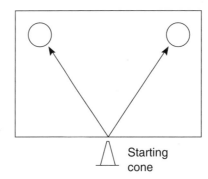

Starting cone

When both teams have played in attacking and defending roles, discuss the game with the children:

How easy is it to score in this two-goal game? (It is harder than in the four-goal game because there are less goals and the same number of defenders.)

What plan did you use as attacking players? (We tried to draw the defenders away from the goal by tempting them to intercept passes made between attacking players near to the goal. If a defender was drawn away from the goal, we passed the ball quickly to an attacker who had moved closer to the goal. Alternatively, if a defender was drawn away from another goal to help at the goal being attacked, the attacking team quickly switched the ball to attack the goal that was left undefended.)

Activity 3: Recognising the Effects of Games Playing on the Body

1. Ask the children to repeat activity 2 and then ask them to consider the effects of playing games on the body. Different teams can be asked to comment on changes that occur in one specific area, such as breathing, heart rate, temperature or appearance.

2. When both teams have played in attacking and defending roles, prompt the teams to share their observations by asking questions:

What happened to the breathing/heart/temperature/appearance as a result of playing games? Why did this happen?

How did you monitor the effects of playing games on the breathing/heart/temperature/appearance?

Give the teams time to discuss their answers before sharing them with the rest of the group. The answers should explain that

- the rate and depth of breathing, monitored by feeling the fall and rise of the chest, increased to provide more oxygen to the working muscles;

- the heart rate, monitored by counting the pulse, increased to pump oxygen to the working muscles;
- the temperature, monitored by feeling the skin and recording personal feelings, increased because the muscles produce energy as heat when they are working; and
- the changes in appearance, monitored by observation of others, could have included the skin becoming flushed because of blood vessels becoming wider and closer to the surface of the skin; and the body sweating to cool down and avoid overheating.

3. If you have time, repeat activity 2 to enable children to think about the effects of games playing on the body and to refine attacking tactics within the game.

Cool-Down

Lead the children in specific stretches for the back of the lower leg (calf), the front of the upper leg (quadriceps) and the back of upper leg (hamstring). These stretches are held still for 10 to 12 seconds.

Conclusion and Assessment Opportunities

Discuss the activity with the children:

From your observations, which parts of the body are going to benefit from playing games? (The muscles, heart and lungs because they are all working hard.)

Will our bones benefit from playing games? How do bones get stronger? (When the muscles work hard they pull on the bone covering and encourage the bones to grow stronger. Any activities which make the muscles work really hard, such as jogging, lifting, pulling, pushing and jumping, will make bones stronger.)

When you are playing games, consider whether any bone-strengthening actions are included.

1. Question the children about the effects of playing games on the body, by drawing individuals out of the game for a short time and asking them any of the questions suggested in the lesson plan.

2. If the observations collected during the games lesson link with a science lesson, you can set preparatory and follow-up work in the classroom which will help to provide evidence of children's understanding. You can talk to individual children about their observations and conclusions.

Preparatory and Follow-Up Ideas

1. You might ask children to record their observations and conclusions concerning the effects of playing games on the body, as part of a scientific investigation. This investigation could start and finish in the classroom, with the games lesson providing an opportunity to make and record observations.

2. In a future games lesson the principle of creating scoring opportunities can be developed further through activity 4.

Activity 4: Creating Scoring Opportunities in a One-Goal/Three-Defender Game

1. The playing area remains the same size as before, but there is one goal at the centre of the widest line, with the starting cone placed opposite it (see figure below). The rules for playing are the same as before.

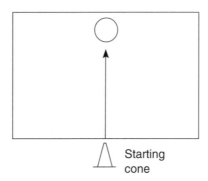

2. Let the children play the game for a short time. Then provide opportunities for the participants to discuss the problem of crowding around the goal, which can decrease the activity level of the game. Challenge them to design a new rule to ensure that the area around the goal does not become crowded. Groups can share their ideas, discuss them with you and try them out in their own games. In this way, children will be involved in evaluating the success of their own ideas.

Solutions to the goal-crowding problem might include:

- Marking an area around the goal into which only certain players from either team can go.
- Drawing a line close to the goal beyond which only certain players from either team can go.
- Either of the above solutions, but with time restrictions for players remaining within the marked area close to the goal.
- The defenders can be drawn away from the goal by awarding one point for every pass made by the attacking team and five points for every goal. In this way, if the goal area is crowded the attacking team can try to score points through passing, and thus draw the defenders away from the goal.

Differentiation

Children with low skill levels or special learning needs may be more successful with activities 1 and 2 if the number of goals is increased to five or six. This will provide more opportunities and more time for the attacking team to score goals. Team numbers can be adjusted to ensure success for the attacking team—three attacking players and two defenders, for example.

During the lesson groups of children may move on to the next development of the game when you perceive that they are ready. This means that different groups can be involved in a range of developments at the same time during the lesson.

Key Stage 2: Teaching HRE Through Outdoor and Adventurous Activities

LEARNING OUTCOMES

HRE: To enable children to explore running activities as a way of being moderately to vigorously active.

Health Education: To enable children to understand that if energy intake is greater than expenditure of energy, the body stores the excess as fat.

Outdoor and Adventurous Activities: To enable children to perform simple orienteering exercises in the school grounds.

Cross-Curricular Links

Geography: Geographical Skills Programme of Study—To enable children to use and interpret maps and plans.

EQUIPMENT

- Simple map of the school grounds (showing positions of buildings, fences, large trees, school entrance, and paths). The map must include numbers 1 to 26 marked in places that can be found easily (see figure on page 84).
- 26 marker cones, showing a number and a letter on a sticky label
- Car Gears and Energy Expenditure chart (see table 6.3 on page 85)
- One Codebreaker sheet per pupil (see tables 6.4 and 6.5 on pages 86-87)
- One pencil per pupil
- One whistle (optional)

Starting the Lesson

Ask the children what they know about energy:

How does a car get the energy it needs to make it go? (From fuel—petrol or diesel.)

Our body needs fuel in the same way as a car needs fuel. What fuel does our body need? (Fuel from food and drink.)

A car uses fuel to make its engine work. What do our bodies use fuel for? (To make energy to jump, run and be active.)

If a car engine is turned on but the car is standing still, is the car using any fuel? (Yes it is, because it needs fuel to keep its engine working.)

When does the car not need any fuel? (When the engine is turned off.)

Although our bodies are like cars in many ways, parts of our bodies are always working even when we are not being active. Our engines are never turned off.

Which parts of your body do you think are always working even when you are just sitting or lying down? (The heart, the brain, the digestive system, and some muscles.)

If a car engine is always working it will use fuel all of the time. In the same way, our bodies use fuel all of the time.

What we are going to do today involves running to search for clues which have been placed in the school grounds. This is an introduction to a sport called orienteering, which involves competitors completing a running trail using a map and, sometimes, a compass.

Performing exercise is similar to taking a car on a journey. What do we have to check before we go on a car journey? (That the car has enough fuel.)

Did you give your body some fuel this morning? Is your body ready to be active?

Warm-Up

1. Show the group a simple map of the school grounds and explain that a cone is going to be placed in each place marked with a number on the map (see figure below). Each cone has a number and a letter written on it (e.g., B6) and must be placed accurately in the position indicated on the map. Ask the children to determine the exact location of number 6.

2. Take cone B6 and jog with the group to the appropriate location in the school grounds. Place the cone on the ground in the correct place, as indicated on the map. Jog with the group back to the starting point.

3. Lead the children through mobility exercises for shoulders, lower spine and upper spine, such as arm circles, side bends and upper-body twists. These exercises should be performed with control.

4. Distribute the remaining 25 cones among the children (one each, or some children working in pairs) and challenge them to place their cone in the correct position in the school grounds, using the map and the number on the cone to locate the appropriate place. Ask them to jog at a steady speed and return to the starting point when they have placed their cone.

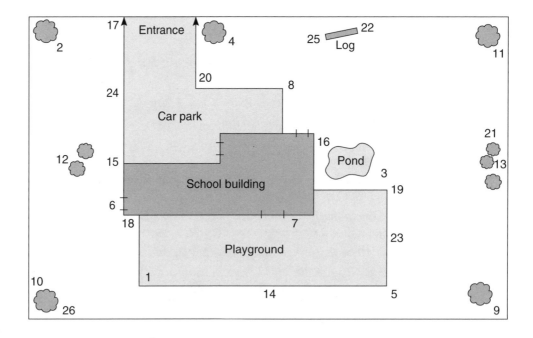

TABLE 6.3 Car Gears and Energy Expenditure Chart	
Car gear	**Energy used**
5	A huge amount
4	A large amount
3	A medium amount
2	A small amount
1	A very small amount
Neutral	A tiny amount

5. When they have completed this activity, lead stretches for the back of the lower leg (calf), the front of the upper leg (quadriceps) and the back of the upper leg (hamstring). Each stretch should be held still for 6 to 10 seconds.

6. Referring to the Car Gears chart (table 6.3), ask the group some questions:

Which gear are we in now? (Neutral.)

How much energy are we using when we are in neutral? (Only a little.)

Which gear were we working in during the warm-up? (First or second gear.)

How much energy were we using during the warm-up? (A little more than when we were standing still.)

In which gear would we be using the most energy? (Top gear.)

How long could we keep working in top gear, our maximum rate? (Not very long.)

We are going to work in third or fourth gear for the next activity, so that we can keep working for about 15 minutes. If you find it hard to keep jogging in third or fourth you can change down a gear, but try not to change to neutral! The exercise should make you huff and puff, but you should not feel worn out.

Activity: Codebreaker

1. Distribute the Codebreaker sheets (see tables 6.4 and 6.5) and the pencils and explain that the aim of the activity is to decode the secret message. Each number on the Codebreaker sheet corresponds to a letter. The first task is to find out which letters correspond to which numbers. This will involve visiting all of the cones the group has placed around the school grounds and noting down the appropriate letter against the number on the top part of their Codebreaker sheet. (Explain that they will be given time to complete the bottom part of the sheet at the end of the lesson, after the cool-down.) Suggest

TABLE 6.4   Codebreaker Sheet

Number	1	2	3	4	5	6	7	8	9	10	11	12	13
Letter													
Number	14	15	16	17	18	19	20	21	22	23	24	25	26
Letter													

Secret message

22	21	26	21	19	23	3	23	19	23	24	2	21	7	1	24	16	19
12	16	22	11		13	19	26	11	5	13	21						
22	21	6	1	26	21	19	23	26	3	23	19	23	24	2	21	23	18	23	19	14	20	23	19
15		13	22	19	1	7	13	9	7	15	18	23					
23	19	24	23	2	21	9	1	22	23	3	4	24	1	22	1	26	

What 'fuel' gives us energy?

If our bodies do not have enough 'fuel' to do all the activities we want to do, how do we feel?

If a car is filled with more fuel than it needs, what happens to the extra fuel?

If our body takes in more 'fuel' than it needs, what happens to the extra 'fuel'?

TABLE 6.5   Codebreaker Teacher's Sheet

Number	1	2	3	4	5	6	7	8	9	10	11	12	13
Letter	O	G	S	F	L	B	T	K	C	Z	P	J	A
Number	14	15	16	17	18	19	20	21	22	23	24	25	26
Letter	W	I	U	X	V	N	H	Y	M	E	R	Q	D

Secret message

22	21	6	1	26	21	19	23	23	26	3	23	19	23	24	2	21
M	Y	B	O	D	Y	N	E	E	D	S	E	N	E	R	G	Y

7	1	24	16	19	12	16	22	11	13	19	26	11	5	13	21
T	O	R	U	N	J	U	M	P	A	N	D	P	L	A	Y

15	13	22	13	9	7	15	18	23	23	18	23	19	14	20	23	19
I	A	M	A	C	T	I	V	E	E	V	E	N	W	H	E	N

23	19	23	24	2	21	9	1	22	23	3	4	24	1	22	4	1	1	26
E	N	E	R	G	Y	C	O	M	E	S	F	R	O	M	F	O	O	D

What 'fuel' gives us energy?

If our bodies do not have enough 'fuel' to do all the activities we want to do, how do we feel?

If a car is filled with more fuel than it needs, what happens to the extra fuel?

If our body takes in more 'fuel' than it needs, what happens to the extra 'fuel'?

that the children refer to the plan of the school grounds to help them to find all of the cones. They can visit the cones in any order, so encourage them to start at different locations. They can work individually or in pairs.

2. When they have collected all the letters the children return to the starting point. They will probably take varying amounts of time to complete this task, so you should be prepared to organise activities for them while they wait for the rest of the group. For example, you could ask them to perform two minutes of a range of simple activities such as skipping, hula hooping or dribbling a ball. Ask them which gear they are working in and how much energy each of the activities uses.

Cool-Down

1. Allocate each pupil a number from 1 to 26. Some children can work in pairs, if necessary. Challenge them to locate and collect the appropriate cone using the map of the school grounds. Ask them to jog or walk briskly (using first or second gear).

2. Lead the children in specific stretches for the back of the lower leg (calf), the front of the upper leg (quadriceps) and the back of the upper leg (hamstring). These stretches should be held still for 10 to 12 seconds.

Conclusion and Assessment Opportunities

Discuss the activity just done with the children:

In our lesson today, how often were you in neutral gear? (Not often.)

Which gears did you work in for most of the time? (Second, third and fourth gear.)

How much energy have you used this lesson? (Lots!)

Quad stretches

We have used up a lot of energy in our lesson because we have been working in a higher gear than neutral.

Now we are going back to the classroom to decode the secret message.

1. During the running activities, use any of the questions included in the lesson plan to ask individual children about their perceived activity levels and energy expenditure. You can also ask individual questions while the children are decoding the message and answering the questions on the sheet.

2. The warm-up activity which involves placing cones in correct locations provides opportunities for self-assessment and teacher assessment of a child's ability to interpret a map or plan.

Preparatory and Follow-Up Ideas

1. The children can be shown the map of the school grounds as part of a geography lesson and taught how to interpret the symbols on it. They could be involved in drawing their own plan of the school grounds.

2. The children decode the message by placing the appropriate letters in the boxes beneath the numbers. This is best done in the classroom.

The secret message is:

MY BODY NEEDS ENERGY TO RUN, JUMP AND PLAY

MY BODY NEEDS ENERGY EVEN WHEN I AM NOT ACTIVE

ENERGY COMES FROM FOOD

Help the children to answer the questions on the Codebreaker sheet:

What fuel gives us energy? (Food and drink.)

If a car does not have enough fuel to finish a journey, what happens to it? (It slows down and then stops.)

If our bodies do not have enough fuel to do all the activities we want to do, how do we feel? (We stop wanting to be active, we feel tired, and lacking in energy.)

If a car is filled with more fuel than it needs, what happens to the extra fuel? (The extra fuel is stored in the car's fuel tank until it is needed.)

How much 'fuel' do we need to do all of the activities that we want to do? (Not too little, not too much, just enough.)

If our body takes in more food and drink than it needs, what happens to the extra fuel? (The body stores the extra fuel until it is needed.)

Where does the body store the extra fuel? (Beneath the skin as fat.)

Differentiation

1. Using the Car Gears and Energy Expenditure chart (table 6.3) encourages children to work at their own level. Encourage any children who may be experiencing difficulties (e.g., those who are overweight or have disabilities or injuries) to walk throughout the activity at a pace which feels comfortable and sustainable.

2. More able children can be challenged to decode the secret message while they are completing the running activities rather than in the two stages suggested. Back in the classroom these pupils can be asked to create their own coded messages while other children are solving the Codebreaker sheet.

Key Stage 2: Teaching About the Effects of Exercise on the Pulse Rate (A Focused Lesson)

LEARNING OUTCOMES

HRE: To help children to understand that muscles need a supply of oxygen to keep working and that the heart rate increases to pump oxygen to the working muscles.

Health Education: To enable children to understand that exercise strengthens the heart.

Cross-Curricular Links

Science: Life Processes and Living Things Programme of Study (Human Organisms)— To enable children to understand a simple model of the structure of the heart and how it acts as a pump, how blood circulates in the body, and the effect of exercise on pulse rate.

Experimental and Investigative Science Programme of Study (Obtaining Evidence)— To teach children to use simple equipment to make careful observations and measurements and to use the results of observations to draw and explain conclusions.

EQUIPMENT

- One skipping rope for every four children
- One football for each child
- 10 traffic cones (chairs can be used)
- Circulatory circuit notices and sticky tape or adhesive
- Stop watches or watches with second hands
- One whistle (optional)
- One Practical Worksheet per child (see page 95)

Starting the Lesson

Ask the children what they remember about their heart rate:

Can you remember what happens to the heart when we exercise? (It beats faster and stronger.)

Today we are going to measure what happens to our heart rate when we exercise.

How can we measure our heart rate? (By counting the number of times it beats.)

How can we do this? (By feeling the pulse at our wrist or neck.)

Just after every heart beat, a pulse can be felt in some blood vessels. It is easiest to feel the pressure of the blood at either the wrist, the neck or directly over the heart. Show the children how to locate the radial (wrist) and carotid (neck) pulses. The pulse count can be taken for 15 seconds to provide an assessment of heart rate.

Help the children to measure their pre-exercise pulse rate while they are sitting down. This can be recorded on the Practical Worksheet on page 95.

Warm-Up

The warm-up will help with understanding how the blood circulates through the body.

1. Set out the circuit shown in the figure below. It can be set out in any outdoor or indoor space where there is enough room for children to travel safely.

2. Assemble the children at the 'muscles' cone and tell them about the activity:

Let's jog on the spot. We are now doing some exercise.

Which parts of our bodies are working hard? (Our muscles.)

What are our muscles using up while they are working? (Energy.)

How do we make energy? (From food and oxygen.)

How does the food and oxygen travel to our muscles? (In the blood.)

We are going to take a journey around the body as if we were travelling in the blood.

3. Lead the group in a brisk walk once around the whole circuit, following the route indicated by the arrows on the diagram.

4. Re-assemble the children at the 'muscles' cone and talk to them again:

Let's march on the spot, keeping our backs straight, lifting our knees up and working our arms. Once again our muscles are using energy because we are exercising. When we exercise our muscles use up food and oxygen.

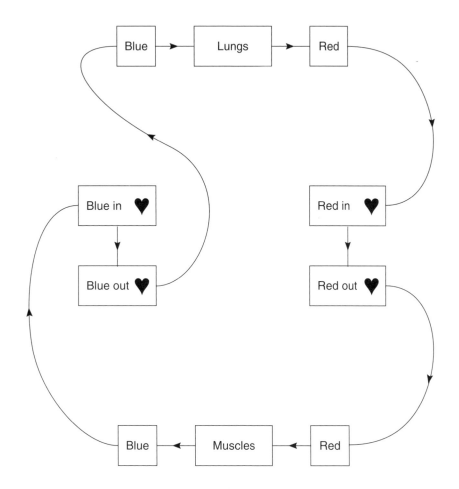

How do our bodies get more food? (By eating and drinking.)

How do our bodies get more oxygen? (By breathing.)

We have used up lots of energy while we have been marching and our blood is low in oxygen, so we must go on a journey to collect more oxygen and bring it back to the muscles. The blue notices on the circuit indicate that the blood is short of oxygen.

What pumps the blood around the body? (The heart.)

Let's go to the heart.

5. The children jog or walk to the blue 'in' cone. Say to them:

We are now in one part of the heart. The heart has four parts. The two top parts collect the blood and the two bottom parts pump it out. We need to go to the bottom part of the heart to be pumped out.

6. The children jog or walk to the blue 'out' cone. Now say:

The blood is about to be pumped out from the heart and it is still short of oxygen. Where do you think it is going to get the oxygen? (From the lungs.)

7. The children jog or walk to the 'lungs' cone. You say:

This is where the blood receives a good supply of oxygen again. How does the oxygen get into the lungs? (We breathe it in through our mouth and nose.)

Let's do some arm circles. Control the circles, make them large and brush your ears with your arms.

Take in a big breath every time your arms go above your head.

Now the blood has lots of oxygen and it is going back to the heart. The heart will pump it back to the muscles.

8. The children jog or walk to the red 'in' cone, to the red 'out' cone, and then back to the 'muscles' cone. Now say:

The notices are now red because the blood is carrying lots of oxygen. The heart collects the blood and pumps it out to the muscles.

9. Lead the group through the journey once again, but this time in a more continuous manner. Ask the children to jog or march on the spot at the 'muscles' cone to represent energy (or oxygen) being used. After this, they should jog to the blue side of the heart and then to the lungs where they perform arm circles and deep breaths to represent oxygen being taken into the body. Then they jog to the red side of the heart and finally to the 'muscles' cone.

10. Ask the children to take partners and complete several laps of the circuit with their partner, starting at different points on the circuit. Encourage them to talk to their partner about their route (saying, 'We are going to the heart to be pumped out to the lungs to collect some oxygen', for example.)

11. When the children are sufficiently warm, lead them in stretches for the back of the lower leg (calf), the front of the upper leg (quadriceps) and the back of the upper leg (hamstring). Each stretch should be held still for 6 to 10 seconds.

Activity: Investigating the Effects of Different Types of Exercise on the Pulse Rate

Divide the children into four groups and ask them to complete three minutes of each of the following exercise activities:

Calf stretches with partner

- Jogging
- Brisk walking
- Football or basketball dribbling
- Skipping

The jogging, walking and dribbling activities can be performed around the circulatory circuit and the skipping activities in a suitable area to the side. If the children are not sufficiently skilled in keeping the ball close to their body when dribbling, they can carry out this activity in a separate space rather than in combination with the jogging and walking.

After each exercise activity, children count their pulse for 15 seconds and record it on their worksheet. Let them work independently of you during this activity, if appropriate.

Cool-Down

Ask the children to walk briskly once around the circulatory circuit and collect the cones on their way. Then lead them in specific stretches for the back of the lower leg (calf), the front of the upper leg (quadriceps) and the back of the upper leg (hamstring). These stretches are held still for 10 to 12 seconds.

Conclusion and Assessment Opportunities

The children discuss the questions on the Practical Worksheet in small groups. They should find that their pulse count increases as the exercise intensity increases (so their

Quad stretches with partner

pulse rate is higher in those activities which feel more demanding to perform). Children should understand that working muscles need a supply of oxygen to keep working. The heart rate increases during exercise to pump oxygen to the working muscles.

1. You can question individual children while they are participating in the exercise activities performed around the circulatory circuit. For example:

Where have you just been? (The lungs.)

What happens to the blood in the lungs? (It collects oxygen.)

Where are you going now? (Back to the 'in' part of the heart.)

2. You can question individual children after the lesson using the results recorded and the questions on their worksheet.

Preparatory and Follow-Up Ideas

1. Encourage the children to record their pulse count at different times during the day. They should find that their pulse count is lowest before they get out of bed in the morning because their metabolism (the rate at which the body uses energy) slows down during sleep.

2. Ask them to draw or copy a drawing of the circulatory circuit and to colour the appropriate parts of the circuit red and blue.

Differentiation

Some children may work independently during the main activity, while other children work more closely with the teacher. The children perform all activities at their own pace and level.

Practical Worksheet
Health-Related Exercise

Topic: Investigating Pulse Rate

What you will need: a pen or pencil and a stopwatch or digital watch

What to do:

1. Find your pulse at your wrist or your neck and count for 15 seconds. Your teacher will show you how to take your pulse.

   Pulse rate before exercise _____

2. Warm up.

3. Spend 3 minutes on each of the following activities. After each one, count your pulse for 15 seconds and write down your results.

Investigating the Effects of Exercise on the Pulse Rate	
Activity	Pulse count/15 secs
1.	
2.	
3.	
4.	

4. Cool down

Things to think about:

1. Which method of taking your pulse do you prefer?
2. Which activity raised your pulse the least? Why do you think this was?
3. Which activity raised your pulse the most? Why do you think this was?
4. Why did your pulse rate change during the lesson?

What to do next:

1. Try to take your pulse at different times of the day:
   - before you get out of bed
   - while travelling to school
   - during a classroom lesson
   - during lunchtime or breaktime
   - after climbing some stairs
2. Try to teach a member of your family to take their own pulse and explain to them what pulse rate measures.

Do you know:

How to find your pulse and count it at 2 different places?

How to make your pulse rate higher or lower?

Why your pulse rate changes during different types of activities?

Key Stage 2: Teaching About the Effects of Exercise on the Body (A Focused Lesson)

LEARNING OUTCOMES

HRE: To enable children to understand that

- muscles need a supply of oxygen to keep working,
- the rate and depth of breathing increases to provide more oxygen to the working muscles,
- the appearance can become flushed because blood vessels become wider and closer to the surface of the skin,
- the temperature increases because the muscles produce energy as heat when they are working, and
- the body sweats when it is very warm to cool down and avoid overheating.

Cross-Curricular Links

Science: Experimental and Investigative Science Programme of Study (Obtaining Evidence)—To teach children to use simple equipment to make careful observations and measurements, and to use the results of observations to draw and explain conclusions.

English: Speaking and Listening Programme of Study (Standard English and English Study)—To extend and enrich children's vocabulary through activities that focus on words and their meanings.

EQUIPMENT

- One Practical Worksheet per pupil (see pages 99-100)
- Equipment will depend on the exercise activities selected for inclusion in the lesson. Equipment lists accompany the activity ideas in chapter 7.

Starting the Lesson

Tell the children:

We are going to investigate what happens to our breathing, temperature and appearance when we exercise and to understand why these changes occur.

Warm-Up

Lead the children through mobility exercises for the shoulders and spine (e.g., arm circles, upper-body twists and side bends). These exercises should be performed with control and repeated six to eight times.

Ask the children to complete two minutes of each of activities 1 to 4 on their Practical Worksheet (see pages 99-100) and write down words to describe how they feel after each activity in the spaces provided on the worksheet. You may direct these four activities, or ask the children to work more independently in pairs or small groups. The idea is that the children will experience a range of activities which gradually become more intense, and to record and discuss the effects of the different activities on their bodies. When they have completed activities 1 to 4, lead them in stretches for the back of the lower leg (calf), the front of the upper leg (quadriceps) and the back of the upper leg (hamstring). Each stretch should be held still for 6 to 10 seconds.

Activity

Lead the children in a continuous activity which lasts for about 10 minutes, or two shorter activities lasting for approximately 5 minutes each. The Card Games or the Active Field / Strike Games described in chapter 7 are suitable for this purpose.

Ask the children to record the effects of these activities in the appropriate box on their worksheets.

Cool-Down

Children complete two minutes of each of the activities 6 and 7 on their practical worksheet, and write down words to describe how they feel after each activity in the space provided.

Lead the children in specific stretches for the back of the lower leg (calf), the front of the upper leg (quadriceps) and the back of the upper leg (hamstring). These stretches are held still for 10 to 12 seconds.

Conclusion and Assessment Opportunities

The children discuss the questions on the Practical Worksheet in small groups or with a partner. They should find that, during exercise

1. the rate and depth of breathing increases to provide more oxygen to the working muscles,

2. their body temperature increases because the muscles produce energy as heat when they are working,

3. the body sweats when it is very warm to cool down and avoid overheating, and

4. the appearance becomes flushed as blood vessels become wider and closer to the surface of the skin.

To assess pupils' understanding you may

1. join in with partner or group discussions concerning the answers to the questions on the worksheet,

2. discuss the answers to the questions on the worksheet with children on an individual basis, or

3. question the children about their observations while they are engaged in activities 1 to 4. For example:

What has happened to your breathing rate now?

Why do you think this has happened?

Preparatory and Follow-Up Ideas

Encourage children to record the effects on their breathing rate, temperature and appearance of different activities completed during one day. A suggested questionnaire is included in the Practical Worksheet shown on pages 99-100.

Differentiation

Some children may work independently during the main activity, while other children work more closely with the teacher. Children perform all activities at their own pace and level.

Practical Worksheet
Health-Related Exercise

Topic: *Investigating the Effects of Exercise on the Breathing Rate, Temperature and Appearance*

What you will need: *a pen or pencil and a stopwatch or digital watch*

What to do:

1. Complete activities 1 to 4 with a partner.
   - How do you feel after each activity?
   - Write down words to describe how you feel in the table on the worksheet.
   - The words shown underneath the table may help you or you can choose your own words.
2. The teacher will lead you through some stretches.
3. You are going to take part in a continuous activity for 10 minutes. Your teacher will tell you what to do.

   How do you feel at the end of the activity? Once again, write it down in the table.

Investigating the Effects of Exercise on the Breathing Rate, Temperature and Appearance	
Activities	**How I felt afterwards**
1. Gentle walk (2 mins)	
2. Brisk walk (2 mins)	
3. Gentle jog (2 mins)	
4. Brisk run (2 mins)	
5. Continuous game or activity (10 mins)	
6. Gentle jog (1 min)	
7. Brisk walk (1 min)	

(continued)

Practical Worksheet (continued)
Health-Related Exercise

Words to help you:

Temperature: warm, sticky, damp, cold, clammy

Breathing: heavy, slow, fast, light, deep, noisy, quiet

Appearance: sweaty, flushed, dry, calm

Things to think about:

Look at your table and answer the following questions:

1. What effect did each activity have on your body?
2. Can you explain the effects of exercise on your temperature?
3. Can you explain the effects of exercise on your breathing?
4. Can you explain the effects of exercise on your appearance?

What to do next:

Keep a diary for a few days and list the activities you do during the day. After each activity write down how you feel.

Activity Diary to Investigate the Effects of Exercise on the Breathing Rate, Temperature and Appearance		
Time	**Activity**	**How I felt afterwards**
e.g., 8.20–8.45 a.m.	Walk to school	Warm, breathing a little faster, OK

Do you know:

Why your breathing rate goes up when you exercise?

Why your body temperature goes up when you exercise?

Why your appearance changes when you exercise?

7 Practical Activities

To be successful across a wide age and ability range (Elbourn and Harris, 1990; Harris and Elbourn, 1991, 1992), practical activities must be

- inclusive (so that all children can participate),
- active (with minimal waiting or queuing), and
- enjoyable.

In designing the activities equity, fairness and choice have been considered. Some activities incorporate problem-solving and a high level of involvement for the children. The aim is to present physical activity in a positive and motivating manner for all children.

The practical activities are presented in two sections: warm-up and cool-down ideas, and main activity ideas. These ideas are not a programme in themselves. They are suitable for use in

- the school curriculum (in PE lessons),
- the extra-curricular programme (during breaks, lunch times, after school),
- promotional events (such as a Healthy Living Week),
- activities outside school (in gardens, play areas or parks),
- youth groups (Brownies, Cubs or junior youth club), and
- children's exercise classes (in village halls, leisure centres or clubs).

Warm-Up and Cool-Down Activities

AREA

For general warm-up or cool-down, any indoor or outdoor area can be used.

EQUIPMENT

- Board or card (optional)
- Marker pens (optional)

Warm-Up

You can direct children through the following activities or, at KS 2, they can follow the guidelines as written up on a board or large card.

1. Jog three laps of the area.

2. Do small knee lifts on the spot and then do large, controlled shoulder circles (three backwards and three forwards).

3. Stand still with hands on waist and do
   - three head tilts (head towards shoulder) to each side,
   - three bends to each side of the body, and
   - three body twists to each side (look behind over your shoulder, but keep hips, knees and feet facing forwards).

4. Jog three laps of the area again and, at the same time, do large, controlled arm circles (backwards and forwards).

5. March on the spot with high knees and high arms (about 20 marches).

6. Stand still and do two stretches for the whole body, one long and tall, and one big and wide. Hold each stretch still for 6 to 10 seconds.

7. Shake out the arms and legs ready for action.

Arm circles

Notes

• This warm-up is suitable for many activities. You could write it out on a large card and place it in a hall or gym for children to follow independently at the beginning of lessons or at the start of lunch time or after school activities.

• You may have to amend the wording to suit the children.

• You can help children to read and interpret the guidelines, as appropriate.

• The repertoire of exercises can be added to as the children's movement vocabulary increases. For example, additional pulse-raising activities such as skipping, sidestepping and galloping could replace or be added to the jogging and marching. Also, as they learn more about specific stretches, such as the calf stretch, these can be added to the guidelines.

Cool-Down

Again, you can direct children through the following activities or they can follow written guidelines.

1. Jog two laps of the area.

2. Do two stretches for the whole body, one long and tall, and one wide. These can be done standing, sitting or lying down. Hold each stretch still for 10 to 12 seconds.

3. Shake out the arm and legs.

Primary Colours Warm-Up and Cool-Down

Area

Any indoor or outdoor area which is large enough to allow free movement from one place to another.

Equipment

• Four large activity cards (as described below)
• Bean bags or small balls (sufficient for one between two children)

Warm-Up

1. Place the activity cards around the room as shown in table 7.1. You can stick them on walls or prop them up on chairs.

2. Introduce the warm-up.
   • The whole group begins at any of the activity cards and performs the first task after you have demonstrated it to them.
   • The second task describes how they are to travel to the next activity card.
   • Once again, demonstrate the travelling action for the children to copy.

TABLE 7.1   *Primary Colours Warm-Up and Cool-Down*

Blue
1. Pass the parcel
2. Run to yellow
3. Stretch

Red
1. Marching
2. Skip to blue
3. Stretch

Yellow
1. Clap hands
2. Giant steps to green
3. Stretch

Green
1. Yes and No!
2. Swim to red
3. Stretch

The tasks are simple ones which will not require much explanation.

- **Pass the parcel**: The children stand back to back with a partner and pass a bean bag or small ball 10 times by twisting at the waist to one side and then to the other.
- **Clap hands**: The children perform 10 claps. These can be performed above their heads, close to the ground, to the side of their body, in front of them or behind their backs. Encourage them to use a variety of claps.
- **Marching**: The children march 10 times on the spot or travelling, lifting their knees high and using their arms. Discourage them from stamping.
- **Yes and No!**: The children nod or shake their heads using large controlled actions in response to five simple questions from you, such as 'Are you breathing faster?' or 'Can you feel your heart working?'
- **Swim to red**: The children walk to the red card and perform any swimming type movements with their arms—breaststroke, butterfly, front crawl or backstroke.
- **Skip to blue**: The children skip (without a rope) to the blue card.
- **Run to yellow**: The children run to the yellow card.
- **Giant steps to green**: The children travel to the green card using very large strides which require them to lift their knees high.

3. The children complete the first two tasks on each of the activity cards with the teacher. This will involve them travelling around the circuit once.

4. When they return to the card where they started, they will perform the third task which tells them to stretch. Lead them in some general whole-body stretches, such as stretching tall or wide. Each stretch should be held still for 6 to 10 seconds. Examples of appropriate stretches are illustrated in table 2.3 on page 17.

Notes

- You will need to lead the whole group through the warm-up several times before allowing more confident groups to proceed with less direction.

- As the children become familiar with the activities included in the circuit and are able to associate the words on the activity cards with the actions they perform, you may be able to allow some groups to try the warm-up independently. A class which is very familiar with this warm-up could be divided into four groups, each group starting at a different colour. That leaves you free to assist children needing help, or to assess individuals.

• The circuit can be performed to a timed tape of 20 seconds of music followed by a 5-second gap. The children perform the first task on each card for the duration of the music and then travel about the room in the way described on the card for a further 20 seconds to music.

• The colours can be indicated on the activity cards, or the cards can be made of the appropriate colour.

Cool-Down

The children can repeat some of the actions on the activity cards, such as the travelling moves and the stretches. They should be encouraged to hold each stretch still for 10 to 12 seconds. Examples of appropriate stretches are illustrated in table 2.3 on page 17.

Traffic Lights Warm-Up and Cool-Down

Area

You can use any indoor or outdoor area which allows the children to move freely around a circuit marked out with cones. The circuit can be fairly large if the space allows.

Equipment

• Traffic lights cards: these can be notices of the appropriate colour, or more elaborate signs if you like (at least two copies of each card are required)
• Cones: the same number of cones as traffic light cards, plus about six extra cones to position in the centre of the working space

Warm-Up

1. Attach the traffic light cards to the cones and position them in a clear circuit formation in the playing area.

2. Lead the whole group around the circuit and explain how the children should respond to each traffic light notice, then lead them through the appropriate activities. For example:
   • **Green:** Jog gently to the next traffic light.
   • **Amber:** Walk briskly to the next traffic light.
   • **Red:** Stop and move the shoulders, neck and spine (simple mobility exercises performed on the spot).

The children travel on from the red traffic light cone when they have moved the shoulders, neck and spine several times. These exercises should be performed in a smooth and controlled manner. You may need to help the children with ideas at this point in the circuit.

3. At any time during the circuit you can call out 'roundabout'. When this happens, the whole group leave the circuit and jog around the central roundabout before returning to their place in the circuit. Encourage the children to jog around the roundabout in a clockwise direction to avoid collisions.

4. When the children are warm, ask the group to stop at the next red traffic light to perform some whole-body stretches, such as stretching tall or wide. Each stretch should be held still for 6 to 10 seconds. Examples of appropriate stretches are illustrated in table 2.3 on page 17.

Notes

• You could allow children who are very familiar with the circuit to start at any traffic light and to travel around the circuit independently. You might need to help some children, especially those performing mobility exercises at the red traffic lights.

• Older children might like to be involved in setting up the circuit and deciding the route that the 'vehicles' will take. They might decide to incorporate other road signs and features (e.g., speed limit signs could determine the intensity at which the children jog, or contraflow signs might involve them swerving to change traffic lanes as they travel to the next traffic light).

• Instead of using cards, you can call out the colours of the traffic lights as the children are travelling around the coned circuit. Give the children time to respond appropriately before the next colour is called out.

Cool-Down

The cool-down does not require the traffic light cards, but the coned circuit remains. Call out 'green' and 'roundabout' more frequently in the initial stages of the cool-down to ensure that the children keep moving. Reduce the exercise intensity gradually by calling out 'amber' more frequently and, in the latter stages, by calling out a mixture of 'amber' and 'red' before the children perform their cool-down stretches (see table 2.3 on page 17). Each stretch should be held still for 10 to 12 seconds.

Runaway Trains Warm-Up and Cool-Down

Area

You can use any indoor or outdoor area which allows children to travel at different speeds.

Equipment

• Six or more cones, skittles or markers.

Warm-Up

1. Space the cones out in the area. Ask the children to form one long line behind you and tell them they are the carriages of a train that is about to go on a journey around the cones. You are the engine of the train. The carriages must keep one behind the other and close together during the journey.

2. The train takes a winding route around the cones, which helps you to maintain verbal, visual and social contact with the children at the back of the line. Begin by walking and gradually change to a slow jog.

3. While the train is travelling, the children can mobilise their shoulders and elbows by performing 'piston-type' movements with their arms. These movements can be made

Runaway train

larger as the train goes 'uphill' or is 'pulling a heavy load', and smaller as it travels on the flat ground. The arm movements can be performed backwards as the train 'goes backwards'.

4. The train can stop from time to time at a station to perform the following:
   - Passengers can climb in and out of the carriages (lifting the knees high to mobilise them).
   - All the children put their hands on their hips and face forwards. Tell them that some heavy luggage has been put on one side of the train. The 'carriages' bend towards this side (mobilising exercise for the lower back). Then repeat this to the other side, and repeat the whole process a few more times.
   - Look back along the platform to see if an imaginary guard is about to signal for the train to leave the station. By holding the waist of the 'carriage' in front, the children should be able to mobilise the upper spine by twisting the top half of their body to look behind them one way and then the other. This process is repeated a few times.

5. After maintaining a steady speed for a few minutes to mobilise the joints, the train can stop in another station to stretch the muscles. This can include general body stretches (such as reaching tall and wide) or more specific stretches for the legs and arms, depending on the level of knowledge and understanding of the children. Each stretch should be held still for 6 to 10 seconds. See table 2.3 on page 17 for examples of appropriate stretches.

6. The train continues on its journey, but this time it becomes a 'runaway train' which involves short bursts of high-speed work. Lead the group and try to follow high-speed work with an 'uphill' walk, before increasing the speed again. This should enable the whole group to stay together.

Notes

- The children can split into two or more 'trains' when they are familiar with the idea of keeping the whole group together and one behind the other. The trains should not collide and should keep out of each other's way.

• Once the children are familiar with all the movements in the warm-up, you can control the trains verbally and tell them what they are doing next; for example, you could say, 'The train is going up a big hill and the pistons are working very hard with large strong movements.'

• When the children are familiar with the warm-up, you can ask one of them to take on the role of the engine and come to the front of the train.

Cool-Down

The train can begin by travelling quite fast and can gradually slow down, by going up imaginary hills and running out of fuel. The train can then stop to stretch out the muscles. These can include general body stretches, such as reaching tall and wide, or more specific stretches for the legs and arms, depending on the level of knowledge and understanding of the children. Each stretch should be held still for 10 to 12 seconds. Examples of appropriate stretches are illustrated in table 2.3 on page 17.

Gears Warm-Up and Cool-Down

Area

You can use any indoor or outdoor space which allows children to travel in a circuit around cones, line markings or grids.

Equipment

• Cones are required if line markings are not available.

Warm-Up

1. Before starting, you should explain to the group that this activity relies on gradually increasing the intensity of the exercise by working through the gears of a car or bicycle. The children must work out for themselves how the exercise should feel to them in each gear.

2. Children should work on their own. They jog around a circuit marked with cones, lines or natural landmarks such as trees or bushes. Call out the number of the gear they should be working in. The children adjust their speed according to the gear you call.

3. At the start of the warm-up you should call out only first or second gears. Suggest that the arms and shoulders are mobilised at the same time (performing shoulder circles while travelling, for example). The mobility exercises should be performed in a smooth, controlled manner.

4. Children need to change to 'neutral' (on the spot) to perform mobility exercises for the spine, neck and hips before going up through the gears again. As the warm-up progresses, third gear can be introduced.

5. When the children are sufficiently warm, stretches can be performed. Each stretch should be held still for 6 to 10 seconds. Examples of appropriate stretches are illustrated in table 2.3 on page 17.

6. After the children have stretched their muscles, you might call out any gear from first to fourth for a short period of time.

Upper-body twist

Notes

1. When children are familiar with the warm-up, you might use additional words such as 'reverse' and 'turbo' to add some humour to the activity.

2. The same warm-up could be conducted over a straight course, as follows:
   - The children pick up a card at one end of the course which indicates the gear that they should use to travel to the other end of the course. Only first and second gear are used at this stage in the warm-up.
   - When they have arrived at the other end of the course they pick up another card and perform the appropriate activity.
   - If they pick up a 'neutral' card, they should remain at the same end of the course and mobilise two joints several times before selecting another card.
   - When they have completed at least six cards, the children should mobilise any joints they did not cover in the first part of the warm-up. They should then stretch out the muscle groups to be used in the main activity. You might need to remind them which muscle groups to include, or direct this part of the warm-up.
   - When the muscles have been stretched, take out the neutral cards and add cards for the higher gear cards. The children continue to select cards from the piles at either end of the track.

3. The same warm-up can be adapted using the names of different modes of transport to indicate the exercise intensity to the children. For example:

- Push bike
- Mountain bike
- Sports car
- Intercity 125

You can ask the group to choose the vehicles they want to include.

Cool-Down

The exercise intensity is gradually decreased by working back down through the gears. Second and third gears can be used in the centre section of the cool-down and first and second gears in the final section. After this, the children perform some of the stretches illustrated in table 2.3 on page 17. Each stretch should be held still for 10 to 12 seconds.

Games Warm-Up and Cool-Down

Area

You can use any large indoor or outdoor area.

Equipment

None

Warm-Up

1. Children walk or jog at a brisk pace to all four corners of the area and back through the centre after visiting each corner.

2. They stop and mobilise the hip and knee joints using exercises such as hip circles and knee lifts (in front and to the side). These should be performed in a smooth, controlled manner.

Knee lifts

3. They jog to the corners again and, at the same time, mobilise the shoulders using exercises such as shoulder lifts and arm circles (backwards and forwards).

4. They stop and mobilise the spine using exercises such as side bends and upper-body twists (keeping the hips facing forwards). These should be performed in a smooth, controlled manner.

5. The children jog up to any line marked on the floor/ground, and pivot away from it. The pivoting can be performed off either foot. Children can pivot away from each other if lines are not available. Encourage them to look up and be aware of the space and each other.

6. Ask them to stretch the groin muscles (inside of upper leg or adductors) and the hamstrings (back of upper leg). Each stretch should be held still for 6 to 10 seconds. Examples of appropriate stretches are illustrated in table 2.3 on page 17.

7. Ask the children to jog forwards and, now and again, perform small dodging actions to the left (pushing off the right foot and taking the body across to the left, for example). They can do this in pairs with children running towards each other and, just before they meet, dodging away from each other (each dodging to their own left, jogging on, turning round and repeating). This can be repeated dodging to the right.

8. Ask them to stretch the calf muscles (back of lower leg) and quadriceps (front of upper leg) individually or using a partner for support, holding each stretch still for 6 to 10 seconds.

9. The children perform two-footed jumps and raise hands into the air (as if catching a ball). This can be performed with a partner, jogging towards each other and both jumping up and clapping hands above head height (adjusting to relative heights).

10. Ask them to accelerate into open spaces and slow down to a jogging pace on arrival.

Notes

• The amount of direction and guidance you have to give will depend on the level of knowledge and understanding of the children.

• Once the stretches have been performed, some of the more energetic ideas can be developed, for instance the 'jumping and clapping' could be developed as a challenge in which individuals count the number of times they perform this with different people in 10 seconds. You can then challenge them to match or improve on their own personal score a second time around.

• You can incorporate games themes, such as footwork, dodging, marking and spacing, into the warm-up to help provide an early focus to the lesson and to use movements relevant to later activities.

• If the game involves upper-body movements such as throwing and catching, it is sensible to include stretches for the chest (pectorals), the triceps (back of the upper arm) and the upper back (trapezius and rhomboids).

• If specific group sizes are required for the activity to follow, towards the end of the warm-up children can be asked to run around and, when a number is called out, to get themselves into groups of the appropriate size, finishing with the number required for the next activity.

Cool-Down

Direct the children through the following activities:

1. Keeping the legs moving, either jog, sidestep or walk. This can involve travelling back to the changing rooms.

2. If desired, stretches for the chest (pectorals), the triceps (back of the upper arm) and upper back (trapezius and rhomboids) can be performed whilst travelling.

Hamstring stretch

3. Stretches for the hamstrings (back of the upper leg), quadriceps (front of the upper leg), calf (back of the lower leg) and groin (inside of the upper leg or adductors) muscles should be performed, where possible, in relaxed and comfortable positions. Each muscle group stretched should be held still for 10 to 12 seconds. Examples of appropriate stretches are illustrated in table 2.3 on page 17.

4. These stretches can be performed outside or in the changing rooms. If they are performed outside on a cold day, intersperse the stretching with jogging or marching to keep the muscles warm. Benches, walls and trees can be used for variety or additional support during stretches.

Lucky Spot Warm-Up and Cool-Down

Area

Any indoor or outdoor area that is large enough to allow children to travel around the perimeter freely.

Equipment

- Tape recorder and taped music (optional)
- Lucky Spot cards. The cards can be A4 or A5 size with a large number on one side and the exercise prescription on the other side (see table 7.2).

TABLE 7.2 Lucky Spot Cards	
Number	Exercise
1	March on the spot with knees high
2	Shoulder circles
3	Sidestepping into the centre and back
4	Hip circles
5	Calf stretch (back of lower leg)
6	Jumping jax (astride jumps)
7	Hopping on the spot
8	Fast walking
9	Head tilts (head towards shoulder)
10	Skipping into the centre and back
11	Arm circles
12	Hamstring stretch (back of upper leg)
13	Side bends
14	Race walking to all four corners and back
15	Easy walking anywhere in the area
16	Quadriceps stretch (front of upper leg)

The Lucky Spot cards should include mobility, pulse-raising/lowering and stretching exercises on separate cards. Make a note of the numbers of the cards which refer to particular elements of the warm-up and cool-down. For example, cards 2, 4, 9, 11 and 13 are mobility exercises. The cards could include diagrams or teaching points if desired.

Warm-Up

1. Place the Lucky Spot cards with the number side uppermost on the floor around the perimeter of the area.

2. Let the children jog around the area for a short while and then ask them to stop. Call out a 'lucky number'. The child who is positioned nearest to this card, or who has picked it up, leads the rest of the group in the activity described on the reverse of the card. You may need to help the less confident members of the group.

3. At first, you should call out only the numbers of the cards relating to mobility and pulse-raising exercises. As soon as the children are considered to have warmed their muscles sufficiently, the cards referring to stretching exercises can also be included. Each stretch should be held still for 6 to 10 seconds. Examples of appropriate stretches are illustrated in table 2.3 on page 17. The children perform the activity until you (or the music) indicate that they should travel around the room again.

Notes

1. You could use music to determine when the children jog around the perimeter. When the music stops, children stop next to a card or pick one up.

2. As the children become more knowledgeable about warming up and cooling down, the Lucky Spot cards can be less specific. They can act as a potential assessment tool in providing evidence of what children know, understand and can do. Less specific Lucky Spot cards might include tasks such as

- mobilise the shoulders,
- raise the pulse while travelling forwards and backwards, or
- stretch the calf muscles (back of lower leg).

Cool-Down

Call out the numbers of cards representing the less energetic travelling activities. After this, call out the card numbers representing stretches. Each stretch should be held still for 10 to 12 seconds and performed, where possible, in comfortable, relaxed positions. Examples of appropriate stretches are illustrated in table 2.3 on page 17.

Card Games

DESCRIPTION

Circuit-type games in which activities are determined by a random selection process using playing cards.

OBJECTIVE

To involve children in continuous exercise circuits comprising various aerobic activities. Children should be encouraged to work at their own level and pace.

AGE RANGE

Suitable for any age range although the equipment and activities may need to be modified accordingly.

AREA

A large indoor or outdoor area.

EQUIPMENT

For most games you will need:

• A pack of playing cards
• Four large suit cards
• Four large cones
• A hoop for cards (or a circle on the floor)
• A tape recorder (optional)

NOTES

1. Picture cards represent the number 12, aces could be either 1 or 20 and the joker could indicate that the performer has to run around the perimeter of the area until they think of a joke suitable to tell you and the rest of the group.

2. You can 'doctor' the cards as appropriate, by removing low numbers, for example.

3. The children carry on with the game for a specific length of time, such as three minutes, or for the duration of a suitable record.

Card Game 1: Random Run

For general information, see box on page 115.

Procedures

Place the playing cards face down in the centre of the area and place the four large cones at different distances from the centre (see figure below). Attach one large suit card to each cone. Children start in the centre by the playing cards. They each look at a playing card: the suit indicates the cone they must run to and the number indicates how many times they should run to the cone and back. After each go, they select another card from the central pile so that there is continuous activity.

Notes

To develop all energy systems, the cones can be different colours and varying distances from the centre and be associated with different tasks. For example:

- **Blue cone (nearest):** Sprint as fast as possible, jog back.
- **Yellow cone:** Run quickly there and back.
- **Orange cone:** Jog steadily to the cone, sprint back very fast.
- **Red cone (furthest):** Jog steadily there and back.

Organise the activity in such a way that collisions do not occur in the centre of the room.

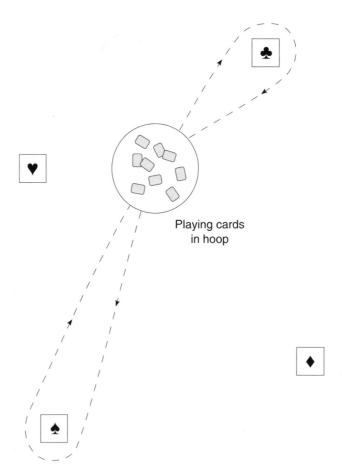

Playing cards
in hoop

Card Game 2: Activity Corners

For general information, see box on page 115.

Procedures

Place the playing cards face down in the centre of the area and place the 4 large cones in the 4 corners/quarters of the area (see figure below). Attach one large suit card to each cone. Each suit card has a different exercise description on it. Children start in the centre by the playing cards. They each look at a playing card: the suit indicates the cone they must run to and the number indicates how many times they should perform the particular exercise on the suit card. After each go, they select another card from the central pile so that there is continuous activity.

Example Activities

Some suitable examples are as follows:
• Jogging laps (hearts)
• Jumping jax or astride jumps (diamonds)
• Step-ups (clubs)
• High knee lifts (spades)

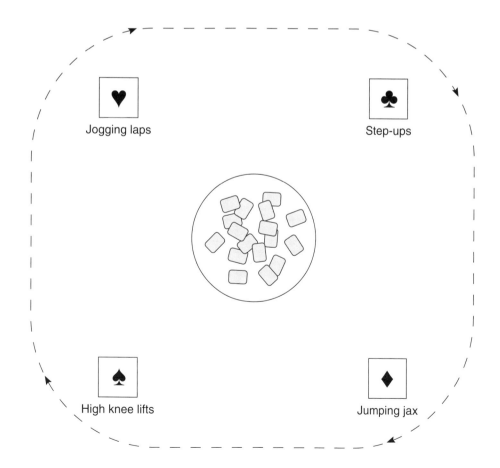

Card Game 3: Skipping Card Game

For general information, see box on page 115.

Equipment

In addition to the equipment listed in the box on page 115, you will need:

• Skipping ropes (one for each child)

Procedures

Place the playing cards face down in the centre of the area and place the 4 large cones in the 4 corners/quarters of the area. Attach one large suit card to each cone. Children start in the centre by the playing cards. They each look at a playing card: the suit corresponds to one or two different skipping skills, and the number indicates how many times they should perform the particular skipping skill. If there is more than one activity on the card, the children can choose which one to perform or can alternate them. After each go, they select another card from the central pile so that there is continuous activity. Less experienced skippers can perform the skills initially without a rope.

Example Skipping Card Game Activities

Some simple examples are

• skipping forwards,
• skipping backwards,
• skipping with both feet together, or
• skipping with feet apart.

Children with more advanced skipping skills can perform

• astride jumps sideways and/or forwards and backwards,
• crosses with feet and/or arms,
• knee lifts and/or can-can, or
• slalom and/or twisters.

Codebreaker Activities

DESCRIPTION

Simple orienteering activities which involve children running between cones to find clues enabling them to solve a problem.

OBJECTIVE

To involve children in fun running activities which also involve problem-solving and strategic planning.

AGE RANGE

Suitable for most age groups. You will obviously need to select the 'messages' and 'jokes' with the audience in mind.

AREA

Any large indoor or outdoor area.

NOTES

1. Children can work in groups of two, three or four. Groups of more than four will reduce the activity level of the group members. Try to ensure that the groups are the same size.

2. The cones are placed at random over a large area but all within sight of the starting point.

3. Some cones may be left blank ('dummy cones').

4. The group members may be given some time to decide how to approach the game tactically—they can split up if they wish or visit cones together.

Codebreaker Activity 1: Basic Codebreaker

For general information, see box on page 119.

Equipment

- 20 to 30 activity cones
- Sticky labels and a marker pen
- A Codebreaker sheet for each group of children
- One pen/pencil per group

Procedures

1. Each cone has a sticky label on the outside with a number written on it, and a sticky label on the inside with a letter written on it.
2. Challenge the groups to 'break the code' by running to the cones and finding out which letters correspond with which numbers. They fill in the appropriate letters on their Codebreaker sheet (see table 7.3).
3. The Codebreaker message might provide the children with a new activity to do as soon as they have broken the code, such as performing 100 skips with a rope or playing Frisbee with their group.

Codebreaker Activity 2: Crackerjoke

For general information, see box on page 119.

Equipment

- 10 to 20 activity cones without labels
- 10 to 15 activity cones with clues attached on the underside
- A Crackerjoke sheet for each group of children
- One pen/pencil per group

Procedures

The procedure is essentially the same as in the basic Codebreaker activity.

1. Approximately half of the cones have sticky labels inside each of which is written one word of the selected joke.
2. Challenge the groups to 'Crackerjoke' by running to the cones and discovering all the words in the joke. They then have to assemble the words in the correct order to reveal the joke.

Example Joke

'What is orange and green and sounds like a parrot? A carrot!'

Jokes of a short question and answer style are particularly suitable, provided that the joke is not a well-known one.

TABLE 7.3 *Example Codebreaker Sheet*

Number	1	2	3	4	5	6	7	8	9	10	11	12	13
Letter													
Number	14	15	16	17	18	19	20	21	22	23	24	25	26
Letter													

11	5	13	21		4	24	15	3	6	23		14	15	7	20	21	1	16	24	2	24	1	16	11

Number	1	2	3	4	5	6	7	8	9	10	11	12	13
Letter	O	G	S	F	L	B	T	K	C	Z	P	J	A
Number	14	15	16	17	18	19	20	21	22	23	24	25	26
Letter	W	I	U	X	V	N	H	Y	M	E	R	Q	D

Codebreaker Activity 3: Crackerdate

For general information, see box on page 119.

Equipment

- 10 to 20 activity cones without labels
- 10 to 15 activity cones with clues attached on the underside
- Crackerdate sheet (see table 7.4) for each group
- One pen/pencil per group

Procedures

1. Approximately half of the cones have sticky labels inside each of which is written a day associated with a particular date, such as St. Valentine's Day or Boxing Day.
2. Challenge the groups to find and solve all the clues by running to the cones and discovering all the days. The answers to all the clues are numbers representing the appropriate day of the month (not the number of the month). The aim of the activity is to add all the answers together to produce the correct total.

TABLE 7.4 Crackerdate Sheet	
Clues	**Answers**
1. St. Valentine's Day	
2. Christmas Day	
3. New Year's Day	
4. VE Day	
5. Shakespeare's birthday	
6. Last day of February (this year)	
7. Last day of this term	
8. First day of next term	
9. 32nd day after May Day	
10. 30th day after Christmas Day	
Total	

Add your answers together to find the total.

Active Field/Strike Games

DESCRIPTION

Simple field/strike games which are active for members of both teams.

OBJECTIVE

To involve children in active games which help develop cardiovascular health (stamina) in addition to field/strike techniques and tactics.

AGE RANGE

Suitable for any age range, although the equipment and rules may need to be modified accordingly.

AREA

Any large indoor or outdoor area. Equipment will need to be adapted for inside use to ensure safety.

Active Strike

For general information, see box above.

Equipment

- Three cones
- One large sponge ball (football size) or an indoor football
- A variety of bats and balls

Procedures

1. The striker kicks, throws or hits the ball as far as possible and then the whole of the striking team (including the striker) run around a cone placed to the side of the playing area and back again to the striking line to score one run (see figure on page 124).
2. The fielder who fields the ball stands still and the rest of the fielding team lines up behind this player. The ball is then passed overhead through each fielder's hands

until it gets to the person at the back of the line. This person then has to run with the ball and place it back on the striking spot.

3. If the fielding team manages to return the ball to the striking spot before every member of the striking team has completed running back to the striking line, the fielding team scores one run and the striking team fails to score.

4. Teams change round when the struck ball is caught in the air, or when every member of the striking team has had a turn at striking.

5. There are numerous variations. For example,
   - the fielders could pass the ball through their legs instead of overhead;
   - the game could continue as soon as the ball is placed back on the striking spot so it becomes almost non-stop; or
   - the ball could be thrown or kicked from a stationary position or bowled at the striker by a co-operative bowler or an opponent.

Much depends on the purpose of the session and the skills and tactics to be highlighted within the field/strike game situation.

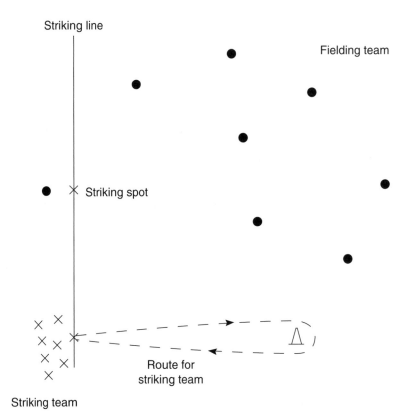

Pick Up Game

For general information, see box on page 123.

Equipment

- Four cones
- At least 12 hoops
- Bean bags, quoits or other suitable objects for collection (at least three per hoop)
- One bucket or box

Procedures

1. The game is played by two teams of nine players or more.
2. At the start of the game, each hoop in the playing area is filled with at least three objects (bean bags, quoits or balls). Three of the fielders position themselves in the playing area and the other fielders remain behind the starting line. One of the striking team prepares to play the ball and the rest of the striking team stands in a group at the edge of the playing area.
3. The striker plays the ball. The choice of ball and method of striking can be altered to suit the ability of the group or individual. The ball can be kicked or thrown by the striker from a point on the starting line, thus requiring no bowler, or a co-operative or opposing bowler can be used and a bat and ball selected.
4. As soon as the ball has been struck, the entire striking team begin to run around the two cones (see figure on page 126). They score one run every time the whole team passes a cone. The striking team continues running until the fielding team has completed its fielding task.
5. The three fielders situated in the playing area field the ball that has been struck and return it to the bucket (or box) as quickly as possible. These three fielders can use throwing and catching skills.
6. As soon as the ball has been returned to the bucket, the whole fielding team can begin its collection task. This involves all the fielders running into the playing area and collecting one object each from any hoop and returning it to the collecting hoops, which are situated behind the starting line at one end of the playing area. Fielders cannot throw the objects to other fielders or into the collecting hoops, they must run with the objects and place them into the collecting hoops. Fielders may only collect one object at a time.
7. As soon as all the objects have been collected, the fielding team shouts 'stop' (or blows a whistle) and the striking team is awarded the appropriate number of runs.

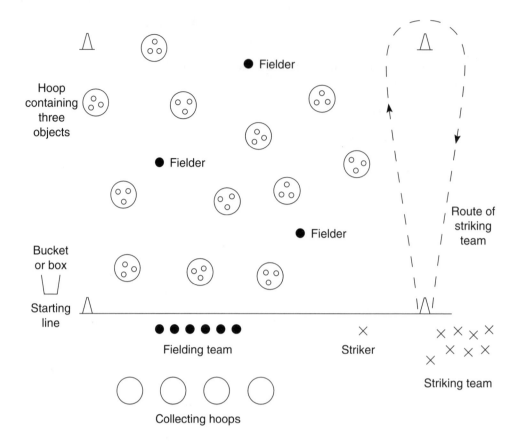

Notes

• The game could be scored in reverse—the fielding team scores the number of objects which it has collected while the striking team completes a specified number of runs.

• A struck ball, when caught, can end an inning.

• If the game is too vigorous for the group (or the weather is hot), the striking team can be permitted to run in two groups with one group resting and one group running per strike of the ball.

Exercise Circuits

DESCRIPTION

Simple circuits in which the exercises have been arranged in a particular sequence and are performed for a specific period of time.

OBJECTIVE

The circuits vary in their purpose. The Odds and Evens Circuit aims to develop the cardiovascular system (stamina). The Whole-Body Circuit aims to develop all round fitness and includes simple low-level muscular strength and endurance exercises interspersed with activities to develop the cardiovascular system.

AGE RANGE

Suitable for the upper end of KS 2. The duration of the stations should be no more than 30 or 45 seconds with inexperienced, unfit or young children.

AREA

Any large indoor area such as a hall, gym or sports hall.

NOTES

1. The focus should be on quality of movement rather than quantity, so it is important to concentrate on good technique rather than speed. Counting should only be introduced once the technique is consistently correct, by which time it should not detract from the performance of the exercises. Performing incorrect push-ups or curl-ups is likely to cause more long-term harm than short-term good.

2. Offer alternatives for each exercise to cater for differing fitness needs.

3. Timed music can be used to control the duration and pacing of the exercises. This frees you from the stopwatch and whistle, giving you time to teach, assist, and motivate.

Exercise Circuit 1: Odds and Evens Circuit

For general information, see box on page 127.

Equipment

- 10 pieces of card to write activities on (five each of two different colours)
- One hoop
- Skipping ropes
- Benches
- Tape recorder and music (optional)
- Recording sheets for children (as desired)

Procedures

1. Place the activity cards with the numbers facing upwards in the hoop in the centre of the playing area. Two hoops of cards can be used for larger groups.
2. If desired, every child can have a recording sheet and a pen or pencil. Children could also work in pairs or small groups.
3. Tell the children that the circuit is composed of activities which promote cardio-vascular health ('heart health') and consists of 10 different activities each of which they will do for 30 seconds.
4. The activities on one set of cards (the red cards, say) tend to be more energetic (of higher intensity) and those on the other set (the blue cards, say) tend to be less energetic (of lower intensity). Children should choose one red card and then one blue card to alternate between very energetic and less energetic activities.
5. They can perform the exercises in any order as long as the different coloured cards are alternated.
6. Explain all the exercises to them and demonstrate safe and correct procedure. It is helpful if the children are already familiar with most of the activities in the circuit.
7. You may not need to designate areas of the space used for certain activities unless the class size is large or the space is limited. Ensure that the children are aware of the need to find sufficient room to allow them to perform their exercises safely.

Example Cards

Some suitable example are given in table 7.5.

Notes

• A warm-up should be performed before the circuit and a cool-down afterwards. During the warm-up, some of the less energetic activities in the circuit can be practised to save time in the circuit explanation.

• It may be preferable to introduce children to a circuit style lesson with fewer activities (six or eight) to reduce the time initially spent on explanations, demonstrations and organisation.

• If music is used, it can be used in the background or as a timed tape. Thirty seconds of lively music, during which the children perform the activity, can be alternated with a gap (of about 15 to 20 seconds) in which children choose a different card and change activities.

TABLE 7.5 Odds and Evens Circuit			
Odd (red) cards		**Even (blue) cards**	
Front	**Reverse**	**Front**	**Reverse**
1	Astride jumps	2	Steady step-ups
3	Skipping	4	Knee to elbow
5	Scissor jumps	6	Quick walking
7	Bench jumps	8	Easy jogging
9	Running	10	Marching

Exercise Circuit 2: Whole-Body Circuit

For general information, see box on page 127.

Equipment

- Tape recorder (optional)
- Prepared music tape (optional): 30 seconds of music with a steady strong beat, a 10- to 15-second gap followed by 30 seconds lively aerobic music and another 10- to 15-second gap (repeated five times)
- Benches
- Skipping ropes

Procedures

1. Prepare the timed tape (if you are using one) and set up the stations with equipment where necessary.
2. Children should warm up using mobility and pulse-raising exercises and short stretches. After completing the circuit they should cool down using pulse-lowering exercises and stretches.
3. Children follow through the stations spending 30 seconds on each one before moving on to the next (see figure on page 130). They perform an aerobic activity at every other station. The aerobic activities are performed in the space between the stations or in the central space. Examples of muscular endurance exercises can be found on pages 20 and 22.

Example Whole-Body Circuit

1. Tummy curls (hands on floor or on legs)
2. Skipping (with or without a rope)
3. Step-ups (on bench with a choice of pace)
4. Fast walking
5. Leg lifts (lying on front, raising alternate legs slowly, head down)

6. Astride jumps (on floor or mat with a choice of pace)
7. Push-ups (against wall or on all fours on floor)
8. Jogging
9. Bench jumps (choice of pace and style—they can place their hands on the bench, for example)
10. Marching

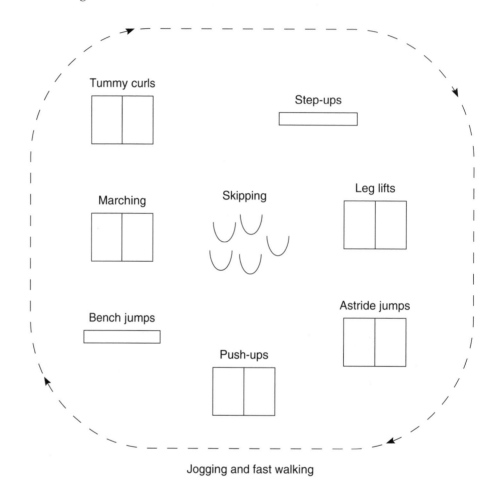

Jogging and fast walking

Miscellaneous Games

Domes and Dishes

Description

An action-reaction game requiring agility.

Objective

To involve children in a fun activity requiring running, agility and quick reactions.

Age Range

Suitable for KS 1 and 2 children.

Area

Any indoor or outdoor area.

Equipment

- About 40 small activity cones to be used as 'domes' and 'dishes'

Procedures

1. The activity is played by two teams. The two teams sit at opposite sides of the playing area.
2. The activity cones are scattered 'dome upwards' over the playing area ('domes').
3. The object of the game is for one team to turn all the 'domes' into 'dishes' by turning them upside down while, at the same time, the other team turn them back and convert them into 'domes'.
4. The activity continues until stopped by the teacher. The number of 'dishes' in the area is counted and recorded. This represents the score for the team converting 'domes' to 'dishes'. The number of 'domes' in the area represents the score for the team converting 'dishes' to 'domes'.
5. The activity cones are returned to 'domes' and the teams reverse roles and repeat the activity.

Going for Gold

Description

This is a development of an activity called 'Capture the Flag' but has several targets rather than one, thus permitting more involvement in scoring. Going for Gold is an invasion game in which one team attempts to enter the opposition's territory and capture 'pieces of gold' whilst trying to prevent their own 'gold' from being captured.

Objective

To provide children with the opportunity to take part in a lively and fast-moving game which promotes running and skipping activities as well as tactical problem-solving.

Age Range

Suitable for most age ranges (KS 2 and beyond). The size of the playing area can be varied accordingly.

Area

Large outdoor playing area, preferably grass.

Equipment

- Six pieces of gold (large stones sprayed gold)
- Six large traffic cones (to put gold under)
- Bands or bibs (one for each child)
- Eight smaller cones (to make two 'prisons')
- Skipping ropes (some for each prison)
- Two different noise makers, such as hooters, whistles or bells

Procedures

1. The game is played by two teams. Each team member has a visible 'tail' (a bib or band tucked into their waistband at the back).
2. The playing area should be split into two equal halves with three cones spread out close to the end line of each territory (see figure on page 133). Each cone conceals a piece of gold. Each team starts in its own territory.
3. The object of the game is to capture the opposition's three pieces of gold. Once a piece of gold is captured by a team and taken back to their own territory, they keep it and the score is 1–0. The scorer signals the capture of the piece of gold using the team's noise maker.
4. The game continues until one team has captured all three pieces of gold belonging to the opposition. This may take anything from five minutes to over an hour!
5. Children can move anywhere, but if a player's tail is removed by one of the opposition (in the opposition's territory) they must go to the opposition's prison (a coned area in the corner of their territory). The tail that is removed is taken to the centre line and left there to be collected when the prisoner is free again. The prisoner can

be released by skipping around the perimeter of the territory and back to the starting point (or back to their own prison, if you think the entire perimeter too far for the particular group or individual). Alternatively, prisoners could perform 100 skips in the area, without the need to travel.

6. You can add further rules later, if necessary. For example, you could make a rule that no one can defend the cones too closely (the cones could be placed within hoops or marked areas which defenders are not allowed to enter). For younger children, it is a good idea to have a rule that players who have gained possession of pieces of gold are permitted to travel back with them to their own territory without risk of losing their own tails or the gold on the way.

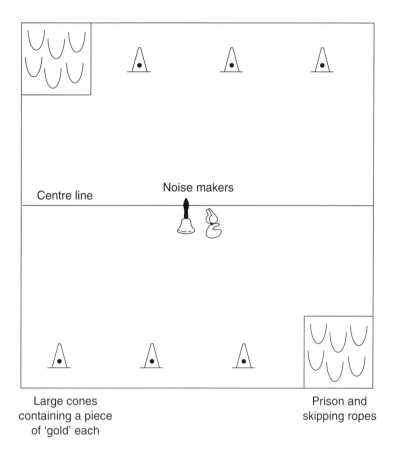

Large cones containing a piece of 'gold' each

Prison and skipping ropes

Waterball

Description

A simplified game of water polo designed to enable swimmers and non-swimmers to contribute to the team effort.

Objective

To involve children in fun exercise in a swimming pool using a game as a stimulus.

Age Range

Suitable for most age ranges (KS 2 and beyond).

Area

A swimming pool of any size.

Equipment

- Three plastic balls (different colours if possible)
- Three hoops

Procedures

1. The game is played by two teams with about six people in each team. The teams may be distinguished by wearing different coloured swimming hats.
2. One hoop is placed at the deep end and the other two hoops are placed in each corner at the shallow end (see figure below). A ball is placed in each of the two hoops in the shallow end. The teacher keeps the third ball.
3. The aim is to score as many points as possible by getting balls into the hoop in the deep end of the pool.
4. The game starts when the teacher throws the third ball into the pool.
5. The team which gains possession of the ball thrown in by the teacher must swop this ball with one of the balls situated in the floating hoops in the shallow end. Once the ball has been swopped, the team in possession attempts to score a goal by getting the ball into the hoop in the deep end.
6. If the defending team regains possession of the ball, it must swop the ball for one in the shallow end before attempting to score a goal.
7. Players may pass the ball or dribble it with their hands. Physical contact should be discouraged.

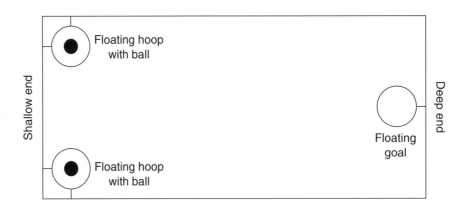

Teaching Resources for Primary Schools

Print Media

Alexander, T., and A. Jackson. 1994. *The FitKid adventure book. Health related fitness for 5 to 14 year olds.* London: Mainstream Publishing.

Armstrong, C.A., P.F. Rosengard, S.A Condon, J.F. Sallis, and R.F. Bernal. 1993. *SPARK (Sports, play and active recreation for kids!) self-management program. Level 2.* San Diego, CA: San Diego State University Foundation.

Biddle, S., and G. Biddle. 1989. Health-related fitness for the primary school. In *Issues in physical education for the primary years,* ed. A. Williams, 54-75. Lewes, East Sussex: The Falmer Press.

Bray, S. 1991. Health-related physical activity in the primary school. In *Issues in physical education,* ed. N. Armstrong and A. Sparkes, 170-89. London: Cassell Educational.

Bray, S. 1993. *Fitness fun. Promoting health in PE.* Crediton, Devon: Southgate Publishers.

British Amateur Gymnastics Association and British Council of Physical Education. 1993. *Persil funfit National Curriculum resource pack for physical education for Key Stages 1 and 2.* Lilleshall: BAGA (assisted by Sportsmatch).

British Heart Foundation. 1994. *At the heart of education. Exercise and heart health. A learning pack for primary schools.* London: British Heart Foundation.

Brodie, D. 1990. *Primary health related fitness programme.* Nottingham: Davies.

Foster, E.R., K. Hartinger, and K.A. Smith. 1992. *Fitness fun. 85 games and activities for children.* Champaign, IL: Human Kinetics.

Goggin, K.J., J.M Williston, P.F Rosengard, R.F. Bernal, and J.F Sallis. 1993. *SPARK (Sports, play and active recreation for kids!) self-management program. Level 1.* San Diego, CA: San Diego State University Foundation.

Harris, J., and J. Elbourn. 1990. *Action for heart health. A practical health related exercise programme for physical education.* Loughborough University, Leicestershire: Exercise and Health Group.

Harris, J., and J. Elbourn.1991. *Further activity ideas for heart health.* Loughborough University, Leicestershire: Exercise and Health Group.

Harris, J., and J. Elbourn. 1992. *Warming up and cooling down. Practical ideas for implementing the physical education National Curriculum.* Loughborough University, Leicestershire: Exercise and Health Group.

Health Education Authority. 1989. *Health for life 1. A teacher's planning guide to health education in the primary school.* Walton-on-Thames, Surrey: Thomas Nelson and Sons.

Health Education Authority. 1989. *Health for life 2. Health education in the primary school. A teacher's guide to three key topics: the world of drugs; keeping myself safe; me and my relationships.* Walton-on-Thames, Surrey: Thomas Nelson and Sons.

Health Education Authority. 1990. *Happy heart 1. Resources for 4 to 7 year olds.* Walton-on-Thames, Surrey: Thomas Nelson and Sons.

Health Education Authority. 1990. *Happy heart 2. Resources for 7 to 11 year olds.* Walton-on-Thames, Surrey: Thomas Nelson and Sons.

Health Education Authority. 1991. *My body. Teachers guide.* Oxford: Heinemann Educational.

Health Education Authority. 1991. *My body. Classroom card pack.* Oxford: Heinemann Educational.

Health Education Authority. 1992. *Happy heart's playground games pack.* Walton-on-Thames, Surrey: Thomas Nelson and Sons.

Hill, S. 1993. *Fitness challenge activity ideas booklet. A resource for playleaders, teachers and coaches.* Hull: University of Hull.

Jackson, L. 1993. *Childsplay. Movement games for fun and fitness. From birth to five.* London: Thorsons.

Kalbfleisch, S. 1987. *Skip to it. The new skipping book.* London: A. and C. Black.

Kalbfleisch, S., J. Harris, and J.Elbourn. 1990. *Skip to health. An instructional programme for fitness leaders.* Ancaster, Canada: Ceta Publishing.

McGeorge, S. 1993. *The exercise challenge.* Loughborough University, Leicestershire: Exercise and Health Group.

McKenzie, T. L., and P. F. Rosengard. 1993. *SPARK (Sports, play and active recreation for kids!) physical education program.* San Diego, CA: San Diego State University Foundation.

Ratliffe, T., and L. M. Ratliffe. 1994. *Teaching children fitness. Becoming a master teacher.* Champaign, IL: Human Kinetics.

Sleap, M. 1990. Promoting health in primary school physical education. In *New directions in physical education,* Volume 1, ed. N. Armstrong, 17-36. Champaign, IL: Human Kinetics.

Sleap, M. 1994. *Fit for life 2. Physical activity sessions for children aged 7–13 years.* Hull: University of Hull.

Sleap, M. 1995. *The very simple skipping ideas book.* Hull: University of Hull.

Sleap, M., and J. Hickman. 1994. *Fit for life 1. Physical activity sessions for children aged 4–9 years.* Hull: University of Hull.

Schwarzenegger, A., and C. Gaines. 1993. *Arnold's fitness for kids. A guide to health, exercise and nutrition.* London: Vermilion Press.

University of Hull. 1994. *Fitness challenge.* University of Hull and Children's World.

Videos

Allied Lyons. 1993. *Backs into the future* (media-mix package: 29 minutes, teacher's manual, posters). Somerset: Hiram Walker Group.

American Master Teacher Program. 1994. *Teaching children fitness* (30 minutes). Champaign, IL: Human Kinetics.

Deane, A. 1992. *Fit 4 kids. Fun exercises for children* (40 minutes). Green Umbrella Productions.

FitClub. 1996. *So you want ideas?* Volume 1 (40 minutes). Dagenham: FitClub International.

FitClub. 1996. *So you want ideas?* Volume 2 (40 minutes). Dagenham: FitClub International.

FitClub USA. 1994. *Captain Hoppy's adventures. Fun fitness for kids aged 5 and up* (40 minutes). FitClub USA.

FitKid. 1993. *FitKid. The fun way to fitness. Health related fitness ideas for kids* (55 minutes). London: FitKid.

FitKid. 1993. *FitKid. Wicked step with FitKid* (55 minutes). London: FitKid

Mattel. 1992. *Dance! workout with Barbie* (30 minutes). Mattel.

Slim Goodbody. 1994. *Step by step for kids. A safe and fun aerobics program* (40 minutes). Champaign, IL: Human Kinetics.

University of Hull. 1994. *Take up the fitness challenge. The fun way to a healthier future.* (5 minutes). Hull: University of Hull and Children's World.

Useful Addresses

British Heart Foundation
Education Department
14 Fitzhardinge Street
London W1H 4DH
Tel: 0171-935-0185

Central YMCA
Training and Development Department
112 Great Russell Street
London WC1B 3NQ
Tel: 0171-580-2989

Children's World Fitness Challenge
CWFC
University of Hull
Hull HU6 7RX

Exercise Association of England Limited
Unit 4, Angel Gate, 326 City Road
London EC1V 2PT
Tel: 0171-278-0811
Fax: 0171-278-0726

Exercise and Health Group
Loughborough University
Loughborough, Leicestershire LE11 3TU
Tel: 01509-223259

Health Education Authority
Hamilton House, Mabledon Place
London WC1H 9TX
Tel: 0171-383-3833

Health Promoting Schools
UK National Co-ordinator
for the European Network of Health Promoting
Schools Project, Young People Section,
Health Education Authority, Hamilton House,
Mabledon Place
London WC1H 9TX

Jump Rope for Heart
National Events Department
British Heart Foundation
14 Fitzhardinge Street
London W1H 4DH

National Back Pain Association
Grundy House
31-33 Park Road
Teddington, Middlesex TW11 OAB

National Coaching Foundation
4 College Close
Beckett Park, Leeds LSU 3QH
Tel: 0113-274-4802
Fax: 0113-275-5019

**Physical Education Association
of the United Kingdom**
10 Churchill Square
West Malling, Kent ME19 4DU
Tel: 01732-875888

Physical Education Association Research Centre
University of Exeter
Exeter EX1 2LU

Research Centre for Physical Education
Exercise and Health, School of Education
University of Hull
Hull HU6 7RX

English Sports Council
16 Upper Woburn Place
London WC1H 0QP
Tel: 071-388-1277
Fax: 071-383-5740

Youth Sport Trust
Rutland Building, Loughborough University,
Loughborough, Leicestershire LE11 3TU
Tel: 01509-228290/1/2

Glossary

Active living: A term used to describe a way of life in which physical activity is valued and integrated into daily life.

Aerobic activity: Activity which uses the large muscles of the body continuously for extended periods of time (e.g., jogging, cycling, swimming, brisk walking, dancing, skipping). During such activity, oxygen supply is plentiful and energy production takes place in the presence of oxygen.

Alignment: The natural position of the bones and ligaments.

Anaerobic activity: Activity which is intensive and is carried out over a short period of time (e.g., 100 metres sprint, long jump). During such activity, the energy demands exceed the body's ability to supply sufficient oxygen. Energy production takes place predominantly in the absence of oxygen.

Ballistic stretching: Uncontrolled bouncing in stretched positions. Not a recommended method of stretching for most people because of its potential to damage the ends of muscles and to cause soreness and stiffness.

Blood pooling: The effect of standing, sitting or lying still after energetic exercise which results in the increased blood circulation collecting in the lower limbs. This can be problematic and can result in a feeling of dizziness.

Cardiovascular endurance: A term associated with the functioning of the cardiovascular system (heart and blood vessels) and its ability to continue exercising over a period of time.

Cardiovascular system: The heart, blood vessels and circulatory system. Also referred to as the cardiorespiratory system.

Carotid pulse: The pulse detected at the carotid artery situated at the side of the neck.

Cool-down: A process which helps the body to recover from exercise safely and comfortably. An effective cool-down should include pulse-lowering exercises and static stretches.

Coronary heart disease: A disease that occurs when the coronary arteries, which supply blood to the heart muscle, become narrowed or blocked.

Duration: The length of time spent exercising.

Exercise: Physical activity undertaken with a specific objective such as the improvement of fitness, performance or health. Participants may follow a recommended exercise programme detailing frequency (how often), intensity (how hard), time/duration (how long) and mode (type) of activity.

Fitness: Ability to perform physical work satisfactorily. Fitness has many components such as cardiovascular endurance, flexibility, strength, agility, speed, power and reaction time. Fitness is specific, fitness for life differing from fitness for sport.

Flexibility: The range of movement around joints. Flexibility is specific to different joints and is improved through mobility exercises and static stretches.

Frequency: The number of times physical activity is performed.

Health: A human condition with physical, social and psychological dimensions. Health can be represented by a continuum ranging from a capacity to enjoy life and to withstand challenges (positive health) to morbidity (disease) and premature mortality (negative health).

Health-related exercise (HRE): Exercise that is associated with health benefits such as an improved ability to perform daily activities and a reduced risk of hypokinetic diseases (those associated with physical inactivity), such as coronary heart disease. Within an educational context, the term HRE refers to the knowledge, understanding, skills and attitudes considered to be essential for the promotion of an active lifestyle.

Heart rate: The number of times the heart beats in a set period of time (e.g., over 15 seconds; over 1 minute).

High-impact activity: Any activity in which both feet leave the floor and the full body weight is absorbed on landing (e.g., jogging, running, jumping, leaping).

Hyperextension: Extreme extension of a joint.

Hyperflexion: Extreme flexion of a joint.

Hypokinetic disease: A disease which can be associated with physical inactivity (e.g., coronary heart disease).

Intensity: This refers to the demands of the exercise on the participant (i.e., how easy or hard the exercise feels).

Lactic acid: A by-product of anaerobic energy production which causes muscle fatigue and soreness.

Loosening up exercises: Controlled movements of the joints through their natural range of movement (e.g., arm circles, knee lifts).

Low-impact activity: Any activity in which one foot remains in contact with the floor (e.g., walking, marching).

Maximum heart rate: The maximum rate at which the heart can function. This can be estimated (over one minute) by subtracting age from 220.

Mobility exercises: Controlled movements of the joints through their natural range of movement (e.g., arm circles, knee lifts).

Moderate intensity activity: Physical activity which feels fairly demanding but not too tiring, and can be sustained for a period of time; 'activity which makes you begin to huff and puff' (e.g., walking, steady jogging).

Muscular endurance: The ability of a muscle (or group of muscles) to work against a resistance repeatedly (e.g., carrying a bench or performing 10 continuous curl-ups).

Muscular strength: The maximum amount of force a muscle (or group of muscles) can exert against a resistance (e.g., lifting a heavy bag or box).

Musculoskeletal system: Bones, joints, muscles, tendons, ligaments and connective tissue.

National Curriculum (NC): The legal requirements for the 5 to 16 school curriculum as detailed within the Education Reform Act 1988 for England and Wales.

Neuromuscular system: The link between the body's nervous and muscular systems (the 'brain-body' link).

Obesity: Excessive amount of body fat.

Osteoporosis: A disease characterised by a reduction in bone mass which increases the risk of fractures.

Overweight: Excess body weight in relation to height.

Perceived exertion: A rating of intensity focusing on how easy or hard exercise feels to an individual.

Physical activity: This is a broad term that describes any body movement produced by skeletal muscles that results in an increase in energy expenditure (over the resting rate). It includes all forms of movement such as routine activities like housework, gardening and walking, as well as exercise and sport.

Physical fitness: A set of attributes that people have or achieve that relates to the ability to perform physical activity. Some fitness components such as speed, co-ordination and power are related to sports performance. Other fitness components are health-related such as cardiorespiratory endurance (stamina), flexibility, muscular strength, muscular endurance, and body composition.

Post-exercise stiffness: The muscular stiffness and soreness which may be experienced immediately after exercise or during the following day(s).

Preparatory stretches: Short static stretches performed in the warm-up to prepare the muscles to be lengthened in the main activity.

Pulmonary system: The lungs and the circulatory system.

Pulse-lowering activities: Rhythmic movements of the large muscle groups that gradually decrease in intensity and help the body to recover from exercise.

Pulse-raising activities: Rhythmic movements of the large muscle groups that gradually increase in intensity and prepare the cardiovascular system for more intensive work.

Pulse rate: The number of times the heart beats over a set period of time (e.g., over 15 seconds; over one minute).

Radial pulse: The pulse detected at the radial artery in the wrist.

Sport: Form of physical activity that involves competition and games.

Stamina: The ability to continue performing aerobic exercise for a reasonable period of time. Also known as heart health, cardiovascular fitness and cardiorespiratory endurance.

Static stretching: Stretches that are held still. Static stretching is recommended as a safe and effective way of lengthening muscle groups and improving flexibility.

Strength: A general term relating to the ability of muscles to exert and sustain force against a resistance.

Suppleness: A general term relating to the range of movement around joints.

Synovial fluid: Lubricating fluid within the inner lining of the joint capsule.

Target zone: The recommended exercise intensity for improving cardiovascular health. Research indicates that for adults this is between 55 percent and 90 percent of maximum heart rate.

Unsafe exercises: Exercises which are likely to incur immediate injury or long-term damage if performed frequently (e.g., standing toe touching). Sometimes referred to as contra-indicated or controversial exercises.

Vigorous intensity activity: Physical activity which feels demanding; 'huff and puff activity' (e.g., running fast, some elements of games playing).

Warming activities: Activities which gradually raise the pulse and warm the body (e.g., walking, marching, jogging). Also known as pulse-raising activities.

Warm-up: A process which involves preparing the body gradually and safely for exercise. An effective warm-up should include mobility and pulse-raising exercises and short static stretches.

References

Almond, L., and S. McGeorge. 1995. *Leicester health—an active schools promotion.* Loughborough University, Leicestershire: Exercise and Health Group.

Almond, L. and V. Morris. 1995. *Lifestyle factors of primary school children.* Paper presented at the Youth Olympics Conference sponsored by Uncle Ben's Rice, Bath, England, July.

Alter, M.J. 1988. *Science of stretching.* Champaign, IL: Human Kinetics.

American Academy of Pediatrics. 1983. Climatic heat stress and the exercising child. *Physician and Sportmedicine* 11: 155-9.

American College of Sports Medicine. 1983. Position statement on proper and improper weight loss programs. *Medicine and Science in Sports and Exercise* 15: ix-xiii.

American College of Sports Medicine. 1988. Opinion statement on physical fitness in children and youth. *Medicine and Science in Sports and Exercise* 20 (4): 422-3.

American College of Sports Medicine. 1991. *Guidelines for exercise testing and prescription.* (4th ed.). Phildelphia, PA: Lea and Febiger.

Armstrong, N. 1989. Children are fit but not active! *Education and Health* 7 (2): 28-32.

Armstrong, N. 1990. Children's physical activity patterns: the implications for physical education. In *New directions in physical education,* Volume 1 , ed. N. Armstrong, 1-15. Champaign, IL: Human Kinetics.

Armstrong, N., and S. Biddle. 1992. Health-related physical activity in the national curriculum. In *New directions in physical education,* Volume 2, ed. N. Armstrong, 71-110. London: Physical Education Association of Great Britain and Northern Ireland.

Armstrong, N., and S. Bray. 1991. Physical activity patterns defined by continuous heart rate monitoring. *Archives of Disease in Childhood* 66: 245-7.

Armstrong, N., and J. Welsman. 1994. Today's children: fitness, fatness, and physical activity. *Education and Health* 12 (5): 65-9.

Armstrong, N., J. Balding, P. Gentle, J. Williams, and B. Kirby. 1990a. Peak oxygen uptake and physical activity in 11- to 16-year olds. *Pediatric Exercise Science* 2: 349-58.

Armstrong, N., J. Balding, P. Gentle, and B. Kirby. 1990b. Patterns of physical activity among 11 to 16 year old British children. *British Medical Journal* 301: 203-5.

Bailey, D. 1989. *R. Tait McKenzie Address,* CAHPER Conference, Halifax, Nova Scotia.

Balding, J. 1994. Asthma update: the problem is increasing. *Education and Health* 12 (4): 63.

Bar-Or, O. 1990. Discussion: growth, exercise, fitness and later outcomes. In *Exercise, fitness and health. A consensus of current knowledge,* ed. C. Bouchard, R.J. Shephard, T. Stephens, J.R. Sutton, and B.D. McPherson, 655-9. Champaign, IL: Human Kinetics.

Bar-Or, O. 1993. Importance of differences between children and adults for exercise testing and exercise prescription. In *Exercise testing and exercise prescription for special cases* (2nd ed.), ed. J.S. Skinner, 57-74. Philadelphia, PA: Lea and Febiger.

Bar-Or, O. 1994. Childhood and adolescent physical activity and fitness and adult risk profile. In *Physical activity, fitness and health. International proceedings and consensus statement,* ed. C. Bouchard, R.J. Shephard, and T. Stephens, 931-942. Champaign, IL: Human Kinetics.

Berenson, G.S., C.A. McMahan, and A.W. Voors, ed. 1980. *Cardiovascular risk factors in children: the early natural history of atherosclerosis and essential hypertension.* New York: Oxford University Press.

Biddle, S. 1991. Teaching weight training. *Bulletin of Physical Education* 27 (1): 34-8.

Biddle, S., and G. Biddle. 1989. Health-related fitness for the primary school. In *Issues in physical education for the primary years,* ed. A. Williams, 54-75. Lewes: The Falmer Press.

Boreham, C.A.G., J.M. Savage, E.D. Primrose, G.W. Cran, C.A. Mahoney, J.J. Strain, and N.M.

Murphy. 1992. Risk factor assessment in school-children: the Northern Ireland 'young hearts' project. *Journal of Sports Sciences*, Conference Communications, 565.

Bouchard, C., R.J. Shephard, and T. Stephens, ed. 1993. *Physical activity, fitness and health. Consensus statement.* Champaign, IL: Human Kinetics.

Bray, S. 1991. Health-related physical activity in the primary school. In *Issues in physical education*, ed. N. Armstrong and A. Sparkes, 170-89. London: Cassell Educational.

Buskirk, E.R. 1993. Obesity. In *Exercise testing and prescription for special cases. Theoretical basis and clinical application* (2nd ed.), ed. J.S. Skinner, 185-210. Philadelphia, PA: Lea and Febiger.

Cale, L., and L. Almond. 1992a. Physical activity levels of young children: a review of the evidence. *Health Education Journal* 51 (2): 94-9.

Cale, L., and L. Almond. 1992b. Children's activity: a review of studies conducted on British children. *Physical Education Review* 15 (2): 111-18.

Cale, L., and J. Harris. 1993. Exercise recommendations for young people. *Physical Education Review* 16 (2): 89-98.

Campbell, W.C. 1994. The school system and active living programs for children and youth. In *Toward active living*, ed. H.A. Quinney, L. Gauvin, and A.E. Wall, 141-5. Champaign, IL: Human Kinetics.

Carruthers, P., A.F. Ebbutt, and G. Barnes. 1995. Teachers' knowledge of asthma and asthma management in primary schools. *Health Education Journal* 54 (1): 28-36.

Central Statistical Office. 1994. *Social Focus on Children*. London: HMSO.

Corbin, C.B., R.P. Pangrazi, and G.J. Welk. 1994. Toward an understanding of appropriate physical activity levels for youth. *Physical Activity and Fitness Research Digest Series* 1 (8): 1-8. President's Council on Physical Fitness and Sports.

Court, J. 1994. Strategies for the management of obesity in children and adolescents. In *Exercise and obesity*, ed. A.P. Hills and M.L. Wahlqvist, 181-93. London: Smith-Gordon.

Curriculum Council for Wales. 1994. A curriculum leader's guide to physical education in the national curriculum at KS1 and KS2. Cardiff: Curriculum Council for Wales.

Curtner-Smith, M.D., W. Chen, and I.G. Kerr. 1995. Health-related fitness in secondary school physical education: a descriptive-analytic study. *Educational Studies* 21 (1): 55-66.

Department for Education. 1995. *Key stages 1 and 2 of the national curriculum.* London: HMSO.

Department for Education and the Welsh Office Education Department. 1995. *Physical education in the national curriculum.* London: HMSO.

Department of Health. 1992. *The health of the nation. A strategy for health in England.* London: HMSO.

Department of Health. 1993. *Health survey for England 1991.* London: HMSO.

Department of Health. 1994. *Health survey for England 1992.* London: HMSO.

Dickenson, B. 1987. *Survey of the activity patterns of young people and their attitudes and perceptions of physical activity and physical education in a local education authority.* Unpublished master's thesis, Loughborough University, Leicestershire.

Dishman, R.K., and A.L. Dunn. 1988. Exercise adherence in children and youth: implications for adulthood. In *Exercise adherence. Its impact on public health*, ed. R.K. Dishman, 155-200. Champaign, IL: Human Kinetics.

Donovan, G., J. McNamara, and P. Gianoli. 1989. *Exercise. Stop. Danger.* Fareham: Fitness Leader Network.

Duda, J.L. 1994. Fostering active living for children and youth: the motivational significance of goal orientations in sport. In *Toward active living*, ed. H.A. Quinney, L. Gauvin, and A.E. Wall, 123-7. Champaign, IL: Human Kinetics.

Duda, J.L., K.R. Fox, S.J.H. Biddle, and N. Armstrong. 1992. Children's achievement goals and beliefs about success in sport. *British Journal of Educational Psychology* 62: 313-23.

Durnin, J.V.G.A. 1992. Physical activity levels past and present. In *Physical activity and health*, ed. N. Morgan, 20-27. Cambridge: Cambridge University Press.

Elbourn, J., and J. Harris, 1990. *Activity ideas for heart health.* (out of print). Loughborough University, Leicestershire: Exercise and Health Group.

Epstein, L.H., J.A. Smith, L.S. Vara, and J.S. Rodefer. 1991. Behavioural economic analysis of activity choice in obese children. *Health Psychology* 10 (5): 311-16.

Fentem, P.H., E.J. Bassey, and N.B. Turnbull. 1988. *The new case for exercise.* London: Sports Council and Health Education Authority.

Fleck, S.J., and Kraemer, W.J. 1987. *Designing resistance training programs.* Champaign, IL: Human Kinetics.

Fox, K.R. 1991. Physical education and its contribution to health and well-being. In *Issues in physical education*, ed. N. Armstrong and A. Sparkes, 123-38. London: Cassell Educational.

Gauvin, L., A.E.T. Wall, and H.A. Quinney. 1994. Physical activity, fitness and health: research and practice. In *Toward active living,* ed. H.A. Quinney, L. Gauvin, and A.E.T. Wall, 1-5. Champaign, IL: Human Kinetics.

Goudas, M., and S. Biddle. 1993. Pupil perceptions of enjoyment in physical education. *Physical Education Review* 16 (2): 145-50.

Grisogono, V. 1984. *Sports injuries. A self-help guide.* London: John Murray.

Harris, J. 1993. Young people's perceptions of health, fitness and exercise. *British Journal of Physical Education Research Supplement* 13: 5-9.

Harris, J. 1994a. Health related exercise in the national curriculum: results of a pilot study in secondary schools. *British Journal of Physical Education Research Supplement* 14: 6-11.

Harris, J. 1994b. Young people's perceptions of health, fitness and exercise: implications for the teaching of health related exercise. *Physical Education Review* 17 (2): 143-51.

Harris, J. 1994c. Physical education in the National Curriculum: is there enough time to be effective? *British Journal of Physical Education* 25 (4): 34-8.

Harris, J. 1995. Physical education: a picture of health? *British Journal of Physical Education* 26 (4): 25-32.

Harris, J., and L. Almond. 1991. Beyond the badge: award systems in physical education. *Strategies,* September, 13-15.

Harris, J., and J. Elbourn. 1991. *Further activity ideas for heart health.* Loughborough University, Leicestershire: Exercise and Health Group.

Harris, J., and J. Elbourn. 1992a. Highlighting health related exercise within the national curriculum—part 1. *British Journal of Physical Education* 23 (1): 18-22.

Harris, J., and J. Elbourn. 1992b. Highlighting health related exercise within the national curriculum—part 2. *British Journal of Physical Education* 23 (2): 5-9.

Harris, J., and J. Elbourn. 1992c. Highlighting health related exercise within the national curriculum—part 3. *British Journal of Physical Education* 23 (3): 4-10.

Harris, J., and J. Elbourn. 1992d. Warming up and cooling down. Loughborough University, Leicestershire: Exercise and Health Group.

Harris, J., and J. Elbourn. 1994. Measure for measure. *Sports Teacher,* Autumn, 11-15.

Hawks, S.R., and P. Richins. 1994. Toward a new paradigm for the management of obesity. *Journal of Health Education* 25 (3): 147-53.

Health Education Authority and Physical Education Association. 1991. Health issues. Exercise for overfat pupils. *Health and Physical Education Project Newsletter* 27: 13-16. Loughborough University, Leicestershire.

Health Education Council and Physical Education Authority. 1986. Health and Physical Education Project. *A health focus in physical education. A collection of case studies.* Loughborough University, Leicestershire: Exercise and Health Group.

Health Promotion Authority for Wales. 1992. *The health promoting school. Progress and future challenges in secondary schools in Wales.* Briefing report No. 2. Cardiff: Health Promotion Authority for Wales.

Hillman, M., J. Adams, and J. Whitelegg. 1990. *One false move.* London: Institute for Policy Studies.

Jones, D.A., and M.E. Mills. 1995. Muscle strength and training in children. In *Sports medicine in childhood and adolescence,* ed. N. Maffulli, 101-8. London: Mosby-Wolfe.

King, J. 1995. Lower limb injuries in adolescence and childhood. In *Sports medicine in childhood and adolescence,* ed. N. Maffulli, 37-50. London: Mosby-Wolfe.

Kraemer, W.J., and S.J. Fleck. 1993. *Strength training for young athletes.* Champaign, IL: Human Kinetics.

Kuh, D.J.L., and C. Cooper. 1992. Physical activity at 36 years: patterns and childhood predictors in a longitudinal study. *Journal of Epidemiology and Community Health* 46: 114-19.

Lee, M.J. 1987. *Coaching children.* Leeds: National Coaching Foundation.

Lefebre, J. 1994. Epidemic of childhood obesity may cause major public health problems, doctor warns. *CAHPER Journal de L'ACSEPl,* Spring, 46-8.

London Central YMCA. 1994. *Getting it right. The Y's guide to safe and effective exercise.* (video: 40 mins.). London: Central YMCA.

Maffulli, N. 1995. Children in sport: questions and controversies. In *Sports medicine in childhood and adolescence,* ed. N. Maffulli, 7-16. London: Mosby-Wolfe.

Malina, R.M. 1990. Growth, exercise, fitness and later outcomes. In *Exercise, fitness and health. A consensus of current knowledge,* ed. C. Bouchard, R.J. Shephard, T. Stephens, J.R. Sutton, and B.D. McPherson. Champaign, IL: Human Kinetics.

Malina, R.M. 1994. Benefits of physical activity from a lifetime perspective. In *Toward active living,* ed. H.A. Quinney, L. Gauvin, and A. E.T. Wall, 47-53. Champaign, IL: Human Kinetics.

Malina, R.M., and C. Bouchard. 1991. *Growth, maturation and physical activity.* Champaign, IL: Human Kinetics.

McGeorge, S. 1990. Special feature—physical activity for those children with asthma or diabetes. In *Health Education Authority and Physical Education Association Health and Physical Education Project Newsletter* 24: 1-6. Loughborough University, Leicestershire.

McGeorge, S. 1993. *The exercise challenge teacher's manual.* Loughborough University, Leicestershire: Exercise and Health Group.

McGeorge, S., L. Almond, and C. Hawkins. 1995. *Physical activity and young people: a review of the literature.* Unpublished internal document. London: Health Education Authority.

McNaught, P. 1986. *Developing flexibility.* Leeds: National Coaching Foundation.

Micheli, L.J. 1986. Pediatric and adolescent sports injuries: recent trends. *Exercise and Sports Science Review* 14 (12): 359-74.

Micheli, L.J., and Klein, J.D. 1991. Sports injuries in children and adolescents. *British Journal of Sports Medicine* 25 (1): 6-9.

Morris, J.N. 1988. In *Children's exercise, health and fitness fact sheet.* London: Sports Council.

Morton, A.R., and K.D. Fitch. 1993. Asthma. In *Exercise testing and prescription for special cases. Theoretical basis and clinical application* (2nd ed.) ed. J.S. Skinner. Philadelphia, PA: Lea and Febiger.

National Association for Sport and Physical Education. 1992. *Developmentally appropriate physical education practices for children.* A position statement of NASPE developed by the Council on Physical Education for Children. Reston, VA: NASPE/AAPHERD.

National Back Pain Association. 1990. *Better backs for children. A guide for teachers and parents.* Middlesex: National Back Pain Association.

National Curriculum Council. 1990. *Curriculum guidance 5. Health education.* York: National Curriculum Council.

National Curriculum Council. 1992. *Physical education non-statutory guidance.* York: National Curriculum Council.

Northern Ireland Curriculum Council. 1994. *The health promoting school. A guide for teachers.* Belfast: Northern Ireland Curriculum Council.

Northern Ireland Fitness Survey. 1989. *The fitness, physical activity, attitudes and lifestyles of Northern Ireland post-primary schoolchildren. A report by the division of physical and health education.* Queen's University of Belfast, Northern Ireland.

Orme, J. 1991. Adolescent girls and exercise: too much of a struggle? *Education and Health* 9 (5): 76-80.

Physical Education Association. 1988. Health-related fitness testing and monitoring in schools. A position statement on behalf of the Physical Education Association by its fitness and health advisory committee. *British Journal of Physical Education* 19 (4/5): 194-5.

Powell, K.E., P.D. Thompson, C.J. Caspersen, and J.S. Kendrick. 1987. Physical activity and the incidence of coronary heart disease. *Annual Review of Public Health* 8: 253-87.

Richardson, J. 1989. *Healthy lifestyles. Promotion events in schools. A set of case studies.* Loughborough University, Leicestershire: HEA Health and Physical Education Project.

Riddoch, C.J., and C.A.G. Boreham. 1995. The health-related physical activity of children. *Sports Medicine* 19 (2): 86-102.

Rowland, T.W. 1990. *Exercise and children's health.* Champaign, IL: Human Kinetics.

Rowland, T.W. 1995. 'The horse is dead; let's dismount.' *Pediatric Exercise Science* 7 (2): 117-20.

Rowley, S. 1992. *Training of young athletes study (TOYA). TOYA and sports injuries.* London: Sports Council.

Royal College of Physicians. 1991. *Medical aspects of exercise. Benefits and risks.* London: Royal College of Physicians.

Safrit, M.J. 1995. *Complete guide to youth fitness testing.* Champaign, IL: Human Kinetics.

Sallis, J.F. 1994. Influences on physical activity of children, adolescents, and adults or determinants of active living. *Physical Activity and Fitness Research Digest* 1 (7): 1-8.

Sallis, J.F., and K. Patrick. 1994a. Physical activity guidelines for adolescents: consensus statement. *Pediatric Exercise Science* 6: 302-14.

Sallis, J.F., and K. Patrick. 1994b. Physical activity guidelines for adolescents: consensus statement. *British Journal of Physical Education Research Supplement* 15: 2-7.

Simons-Morton, B.G., G.S. Parcel, N.M. O'Hara, S.N. Blair, and R.R. Pate. 1988. Health-related physical fitness in childhood: status and recommendations. *Annual Review of Public Health* 9: 403-25.

Sleap, M. 1990. Promoting health in primary school physical education. In *New directions in physical education,* Volume 1, ed. N. Armstrong, 17-36. Champaign, IL: Human Kinetics.

Sleap, M., and P. Warburton. 1992. Physical activity levels of 5-11 year old children in England as determined by continuous observation. *Research Quarterly for Exercise and Sport* 63 (3): 238-45.

Sports Council. 1993. *Young people and sport. Policy and frameworks for action.* London: Sports Council.

Sports Council. 1995. *Young people and sport. National survey selected findings.* London: Sports Council.

Sports Council and Health Education Authority. 1992a. *Allied Dunbar national fitness survey. Main findings.* London: Sports Council and Health Education Authority.

Sports Council and Health Education Authority. 1992b. *Allied Dunbar national fitness survey. A summary of the major findings and messages from the Allied Dunbar national fitness survey.* London: Sports Council and Health Education Authority.

Sports Council for Wales. 1987. *Exercise for health—health-related fitness in Wales.* Heartbeat Report 23. Cardiff: Sports Council for Wales.

Sports Council for Wales. 1993. *Children's sport participation 1991/93.* Cardiff: Sports Council for Wales.

Sports Council for Wales. 1994. *A matter of fun and games: children's participation in sport.* Cardiff: Sports Council for Wales.

Taylor, P. 1995. Foot injuries. In *Sports medicine in childhood and adolescence,* ed. N. Maffulli, 17-25. London: Mosby-Wolfe.

Taylor, W.C., S.N. Blair, S.A Snider, and C.C.C. Wun. 1993. The influence of physical activity in childhood and adolescence on adult exercise habits. *Pediatric Exercise Science* 5: 198-9.

Taylor, W.C., T. Baranowski, and J.F. Sallis. 1994. Family determinants of childhood physical activity: a social-cognitive model. In *Advances in exercise adherence,* ed. R.K. Dishman, 319-42. Champaign, IL: Human Kinetics.

University of Hull. 1994a. *Fitness challenge.* The University of Hull and Children's World.

University of Hull. 1994b. *Take up the fitness challenge. The fun way to a healthier future.* (video). University of Hull and Children's World.

Wankel, L.M., and P.S.J. Kreisel. 1985. Factors underlying enjoyment of youth sports: sport and age group comparisons. *Journal of Sport and Exercise Psychology* 11: 355-66.

Warren, M.P. 1980. The effects of exercise on pubertal progression and reproduction function in girls. *Journal of Clinical Endocrinology and Metabolism* 51 (11): 1150-7.

Wessex Institute of Public Health Medicine and Hampshire County Council Education Department. 1993. *Healthy schools award.* Wessex and Hampshire: Wessex Institute of Public Health Medicine and Hampshire County Council Education Department.

Whitehead, J. 1993. Why children choose to do sport—or stop. In *Coaching children in sport. Principles and practice,* ed. M. Lee, 109-121. London: E. and F.N. Spon.

Williams, A. 1988. Physical activity patterns among adolescents—some curriculum implications. *Physical Education Review* 11 (1): 28-39.

YMCA of the USA. 1994. *YMCA healthy back book.* Champaign, IL: Human Kinetics.

Zwiren, L.D. 1988. Exercise prescription for children. In *Resource manual for guidelines for exercise testing and prescription,* ed. American College of Sports Medicine, 309-14. Philadelphia, PA: Lea and Febiger.

About the Authors

Jill Elbourn and Jo Harris

Jo Harris and Jill Elbourn have played significant roles in the health-related exercise movement in Britain. From 1987 to 1993 they were involved in the "Health and Physical Education" national project at Loughborough University, actively promoting the teaching of health-related exercise in schools across the country.

Since 1988 they have been delivering in-service training courses in health-related exercise for primary and secondary school teachers. Harris and Elbourn have also collaborated on several health-related exercise books and articles, including *Action for Heart Health, Further Activity Ideas for Heart Health* and "Warming Up and Cooling Down."

A lecturer in physical education at Loughborough University since 1990, Harris previously was involved in teacher education in Cheltenham for two years and taught physical education and health education at the secondary school level for twelve years. From 1990 to 1994 she co-directed the Loughborough Summer School Course "Health-Related Exercise in the National Curriculum". She holds a master's degree in physical education from Birmingham University and a PhD in pedagogy, exercise and children's health.

Elbourn is a freelance educational exercise consultant and a part-time lecturer at Loughborough University and other institutions. She also has twelve years' experience in teaching physical education at the secondary school level, and she co-directed the Loughborough Summer School Course "Health-Related Exercise in the National Curriculum" from 1990 to 1994. Elbourn, who holds a bachelor's degree in physical education and social administration from London University, in 1999 will earn her master's degree in physical education from Loughborough University.

Fresh ideas for health-related exercise programmes

Lorraine Barbarash

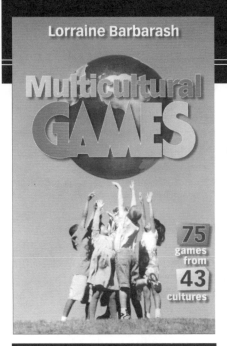

Multicultural GAMES

75 games from 43 cultures

1997 • Paper • 152 pp
Item BBAR0565
ISBN 0-88011-565-3
£12.50

Featuring 75 games from 43 cultures on 6 continents, this practical reference is an excellent source for ideas on building an interdisciplinary and multicultural curriculum. With these activities, your students will develop an appreciation for other cultures while enjoying physical activity.

PARACHUTE GAMES

Todd Strong / Dale LeFevre

1996 • Paper • 168 pp
Item BSTR0793
ISBN 0-87322-793-X
£12.50

Parachute Games will help you revitalise your programmes and involve participants in exciting, easy-to-do activities. With 60 parachute games and 120 accompanying photos, it's a fresh source of ideas that will provide hours of fun and improve the quality of learning in all your activity programmes.

TEAM BUILDING THROUGH PHYSICAL CHALLENGES

DONALD R. GLOVER / DANIEL W. MIDURA

1992 • Paper • 160 pp
Item BGLO0359
ISBN 0-87322-359-4
£13.95

Watch students develop self-confidence and new skills as they explore these 22 physical challenges. Not only will they improve motor skills; they'll learn to value teamwork, practise leadership skills, improve listening skills, and appreciate individual differences—skills that will benefit them throughout their lives.

30-day money-back guarantee!

Prices subject to change.

Human Kinetics
The Information Leader in Physical Activity
http://www.humankinetics.com/
2335